Foreign Policy and Security of India

Foreign Policy and Security of India

Edited by

Josukutty C.A.
Assistant Professor and Honorary Director,
Survey Research Centre, Department of Political Science,
University of Kerala

and

J. Prabhash
Department of Political Science and Formerly
Pro-Vice Chancellor and Director,
School of Social Sciences,
University of Kerala

New Century Publications
New Delhi, India

NEW CENTURY PUBLICATIONS
4800 / 24, Bharat Ram Road,
Ansari Road, Daryaganj,
New Delhi - 110 002 (India)

Tel.: 011-2324 7798, 4358 7398, 4101 7798
E-mail: indiatax@vsnl.com • info@newcenturypublications.com
www.newcenturypublications.com

Editorial office:
LG – 7, Aakarshan Bhawan,
4754-57/23, Ansari Road, Daryaganj,
New Delhi – 110 002

Tel.: 011-4356 0919

First Published: **2017**

ISBN: **978-81-7708-447-4**

Published by New Century Publications and printed at Milan Enterprises, New Delhi.

Designs: Patch Creative Unit, New Delhi.

PRINTED IN INDIA

About the Book

In the early days of India's independence, and in the absence of economic and political clout, India emphasized its civilisational and ideational properties to get visibility in world politics. However, the second most populous country in the world with a functioning democracy was kept out of the high tables of international politics by the big powers. The situation began to change with the end of Cold War when India registered impressive economic growth. The emergence of India as an increasingly influential power in international politics is a remarkable feature of the contemporary global system. Nations across the world—big and small—consider India an attractive partner and want to strengthen their relationship with it. India is spreading its wings to all parts of the world to consolidate its growing position as a pre-eminent power.

India's ambition to become a great power depends upon the careful formulation of its foreign policy strategies and perspectives. A systematic and thoughtful choreographing of India's foreign policy is essential to realise its ambition to become a great power. Issues of cyber security, terrorism, maritime security and climate change need to be tackled with extra care at all levels.

A country should have not only the ambition and capacity to become a great power but also the ability to shape and mould the behaviour of other states in a way that suits its interests. No country is destined to be a great power without working towards it. The consolidation of India's position and great power status depends on the pursuance of its foreign policy through the 21st century.

This book consists of 12 scholarly papers, authored by experts in the field, which provide deep insights into various aspects and dimensions of India's foreign policy.

About the Editors

Dr. Josukutty C.A. is currently Assistant Professor and Honorary Director, Survey Research Centre, Department of Political Science, University of Kerala. He received his M.A. (Political Science), M.Phil. and Ph.D. degrees from the University of Kerala. He was a fellow of the Salzburg Global Seminar (2007) and was selected to study at the United States Institute on U.S. Foreign Policy at the University of Florida, US in 2010. In 2015, he was awarded the Fulbright Nehru Academic and Professional Excellence Fellowship and taught a semester course on India's foreign policy at the University of South Dakota, Vermillion, US.

Dr. Josukutty has to his credit 2 books and more than 60 research and popular articles. He has participated and presented papers in a number of national and international conferences and seminars. He has been serving as General Secretary, Association of Political Scientists, Kerala since 2011. His areas of interest and research include international relations, India's foreign policy, Indo-US relations, electoral politics, and human rights.

Professor J. Prabhash presently teaches Political Science at the University of Kerala and is the former Pro-Vice Chancellor (2009-2013) and Director of School of Social Sciences (2013-2015) of the University. He also worked as Adjunct Professor (2004) at the School of Politics and Economics, Claremont Graduate University, California, US. He was a visiting research fellow (2010-2013) at New South Wales University, Sydney, Australia. He was also the Director General (2008-09) of the Institute of Parliamentary Affairs, Government of Kerala, Thiruvananthapuram. He has published 208 research and popular articles and 3 research monographs.

Contents

Contributors

M.J. Vinod	Professor, Department of Political Science, Bangalore University, Bengaluru, Karnataka.
Monish Tourangbam	Assistant Professor, Department of Geopolitics and International Relations, Manipal University, Manipal, Karnataka.
W. Lawrence S. Prabhakar	Associate Professor, Department of Political Science, Madras Christian College, Chennai, Tamil Nadu.
Suratha Kumar Malik	Assistant Professor, Department of Political Science, Vidyasagar University, Midnapore, West Bengal.
Ramanuj Hazarika	Research Scholar, School of International Studies, Jawaharlal Nehru University (JNU), New Delhi.
Suresh K.	Assistant Professor, University College, Thiruvananthapuram, Kerala.
Baljit Singh	Professor, Department of Political Science, University of Jammu, Jammu.
Shubhi Misra	Research Scholar, Political Geography Division, Centre for International Politics, Organization and Disarmament, Jawaharlal Nehru University (JNU), New Delhi.
Jabin T. Jacob	Assistant Director, Institute of Chinese Studies, Delhi.
Josukutty C.A.	Assistant Professor, Department of Political Science, University of Kerala, Thiruvananthapuram, Kerala.

Anil Kumar P. Assistant Professor, Department of Political Science, University College, Thiruvanthapuram, Kerala.

A. Subramanyam Raju Centre Head and Associate Professor, UNESCO Madanjeet Singh Institute of South Asia Regional Co-operation, Pondicherry University, Puducherry.

Introduction

By the Editors

India is increasingly becoming a powerful and influential state in world politics. For the first time since Independence in 1947, the policymakers and general public alike expect that India could play a major role in international relations. A major reason for such a heightened expectation is the impressive economic growth that the country has registered in recent years. With a stable government at the Centre, many consider this as the most opportune moment for India to initiate productive foreign policy initiatives to achieve its national interests. It has been widely criticized that India does not have a long-term foreign policy strategy. There are differences over the success of non-alignment as a strategy and its contribution to the protection of India's long-term interests. At the same time, the fact that India was not considered as a great power to reckon with during the Cold War days was undisputed. In the post-Cold War period, despite the presence of many favourable factors, there has been a certain reluctance or ambivalence to carve out a clear role for India in international affairs.

International politics is undergoing major transitions economically, politically and diplomatically with far reaching consequences for the future of the world system. India should calibrate appropriate strategies—both theoretical and pragmatic—to take advantage of these transformations. What ideas and theoretical orientations should guide India's foreign policy? Should it follow an independent foreign policy guided by *strategic autonomy*? Will strategic autonomy enable India to break into the ranks of great powers of the 21st century? How far is India's vision of a multilateral, all inclusive, peaceful and non-hegemonic world order, conducive to achieving great power status?

Equally important is the pragmatic management of its relationship with various state and non-state actors. The rise of Asia with China on the lead and the relative decline of the US have a definite impact on India's relationship with its immediate and extended neighbours, great powers, regional and international organizations and other significant actors.

Why are India's neighbours so suspicious and hostile, despite India being very generous and accommodative to them? A lot of balancing and strategy is required to manage the relationship with Pakistan, China and the US. Indian Ocean and Southeast Asia are supremely important as they are the most economically vibrant and politically volatile cites in international relations. Indo-US relationship is very comprehensive and strategic, particularly in the context of *Asian rebalancing* and emerging world order and security threats.

A country should have not only the ambition and capacity to become a great power but also the ability to shape and mould the behaviour of other states in a way that suits its interests. No country is destined to be a great power without working towards it. The consolidation of India's position and great power status depends on what foreign policy India will follow and adopt through the 21st century.

This book is a collection of 12 scholarly papers that discusses various aspects and dimensions of India's foreign policy.

The paper titled *Theoretical Foundations of India's Foreign Policy* by M.J. Vinod strives to identify various modes, premises and arguments germane to a theoretical understanding of contemporary Indian foreign policy. In the paper, he dwells on the Nehruvian, neo-liberal, hyper-realist and regionalists schools of foreign policy perspectives and examines how these perspectives intersect with India's nuclear policy in terms of commonalities and differences. He argues that the foreign policy orientation of the current ruling dispensation at the centre is a mixture of different theoretical positions with a definite predominance for realpolitik *pragmatism.*

The overarching presence of the concept of strategic autonomy is the topic of discussion by Monish Tourangbam in his paper titled *India's Foreign Policy and Strategic Autonomy.* The concept of strategic autonomy has been a guiding star in the evolution of independent India's foreign policy. Even as a newly independent country, facing daunting internal and external challenges, India attempted to define its own path in international affairs. India's decision not to join either of the two blocs brought its fair share of trials in terms of balancing its ties with the United States and the Soviet Union or their allies. With the end of the Cold War and the onset of India's economic liberalisation, India has opened its doors to Western countries, more specifically the United States in ways unthinkable during the Cold War. Presently, as the spectre of a rising China becomes ubiquitous across the spectrum leading to security concerns—accruing out of the possibility of a rising hegemon in the eastern hemisphere—India and the United States or for that matter, America's allies like Japan and Australia sharing similar concerns are engaging in ways hitherto unseen. India is undergoing a transition of its identity, from being seen as a *voice of the voiceless* to aspiring great power status, which takes into account the perceptions of other countries, especially other major powers as to where India stands in the international system. The author soberly and critically analyses the relevance and significance of strategic autonomy in the context of the changing trajectory of India's foreign policy.

In his paper titled *India and the Changing Contexts of Deterrence,* W. Lawrence S. Prabhakar discusses the concept and the theories of deterrence in relation to India's national security strategies. He says that in the context of India's national security policy, and in terms of its evolution and contexts, deterrence plays a pivotal role in the determination of its national security strategy. He contextualizes and analyses the contexts of India's deterrence from the perspectives of multi-tier threat perceptions which include threat of terrorist or asymmetric attacks, limited war, conventional war with conventional deterrence and final stage of resorting to nuclear weapons. He further proceeds to locate the contexts of India's vistas of deterrence. In summation, he argues that India's deterrence has gradually shifted from conventional to nuclear and to the asymmetric as the threats and challenges have changed from conventional war to asymmetric conflicts in the backdrop of nuclear weapons in the subcontinent.

Suratha Kumar Malik in his paper *India's Nuclear Strategy: An Analysis,* critically looks at India's nuclear policy. According to him, *minimum credible nuclear deterrence* doctrine and *no first use* policy are based on the concept of deterrence by denial, rather than deterrence by punishment. Across the entire spectrum of conventional conflict, the first use of nuclear weapons by India does not make sound strategic sense. The real distinguishing feature of India's nuclear doctrine is that it is anchored in India's continued commitment to global, verifiable and non-discriminating nuclear disarmament. The persistence of restraint, stability and minimalism in India's nuclear policy is best explained with reference to its strategic culture. An examination of Indian strategic culture with respect to nuclear weapons by the author reveals: (a) high levels of continuity in the form of restrained responses to external and domestic pressures for change, and in a positive disposition toward arms control; and (b) a significant shift from high to low tolerance of ambiguity resulting from the steady growth of an operational, as opposed to a political, conception of nuclear weapons.

Ramanuj Hazarika in his paper *Soft Power and Public Diplomacy in Foreign Policy of India,* examines the role of soft power in the transformation of India as an emerging world power. This paper discusses the soft power resources of India, what role it has to play in the transformation of India as a major power and how India has been trying to use various public diplomacy initiatives to wield its soft power resources. He investigates the limitations of Indian soft power and public diplomacy initiatives and how can India overcome these difficulties.

Suresh K. in his paper *India's Foreign Policy and Regional Multilateralism* in *South Asia,* discusses the significance of regional economic organizations in social and economic development and political pacification in South Asia. With a shared history and cultural experiences, South Asia has huge potential for economic co-operation and political integration.

However, regional political discords and distrust have neutralized most of the initiatives towards regional cooperation and development. The paper explores the impact of India's foreign policy on development and institutionalization of regional multilaterism in South Asia. The paper tries to answer whether economic compulsions would lead the region to greater economic and political integration and if so what role India can play and to what extent the countries could achieve economic integration despite political hostilities.

Baljit Singh in his paper *India and the Evolving Power Structure in Southeast Asia*, analyses the evolving security scenario in Southeast Asia and stakes for India. India is up to consolidate its position in the Southeast Asian region through economic and naval diplomacy. In the strategic domain, the ASEAN countries are looking towards India not only as a reliable security partner but also as a state having acquired naval capability to moderate growing Chinese influence in this region.

Shubhi Misra in the paper titled *India's Prospects in BRICS,* looks at BRICS from a critical perspective and appraises how coherent the forum is as a player in the international realm. The coming together of these countries has both geo-economic as well as geo-political underpinnings. The first part of the paper discusses the escalating co-operation between the developing countries where it talks about how individual states are benefited by entering into alliances while the second part talks about the BRICS, its development bank and its reserved funds. China has evolved tremendously and its role in the world and also in the multilateral forum like these cannot be overlooked. The last part of the paper tries to locate India's individual interest amidst the widening scope of BRICS and its bilateral ties with the West.

Jabin T. Jacob in the paper titled *China's 'New Tianxia' Strategy and the Indian Response*, focuses on China's new foreign policy initiatives to draw the Asian continent first and then further afield into an ever closer economic and political relationship with China. Two parts of this form of Chinese foreign policy are examined in this paper—one, China's frequent hosting of international conferences and seminars and two, its promotion of new ideas and new organizations as a way of shaping a common narrative for Asia, with China in the lead. Alongside, this paper also highlights how India lags behind China in terms of organizing principles and institutional capabilities. The author concludes that China is harking back to ancient principles and the worldviews of an imperial power as a framework for its foreign policy that continues to evolve in a world where its economic power is growing stronger.

Josukutty C.A. in his paper *Constraints in Indo-US Relations amidst Growing Bonhomie,* looks at the constraints in Indo-US relations. The key argument of the paper is that despite the growing camaraderie between India and the US, there are many fundamental differences that can derail and adversely affect the prospects of mutual co-operation. The persisting US military and economic aid to Pakistan, chinks in the joint fight against terrorism, lack of concern on the part of the US towards India's security threats at the borders with Pakistan and China are issues that run counter to the core interests of India. Indian advocacy of an inclusive multilateral world order and adherence to independence in foreign policy limit the deepening of the relationship beyond the rhetoric of a strategic partnership.

Anil Kumar P. in his paper *India's Soft Balancing with US and China,* explains the nuances of balancing India's strategic alliance with the US and competition with China. The idea of resisting the stronger one and maximising the national interest touches upon the work of political realists who argue that states in the post-Cold War era are balancing against the unipolar might or the stronger one is not in the traditional sense of using military build-ups, war-fighting alliances, or transfers to military opponents. Instead, it is through *soft balancing,* in which states leverage international institutions, economic statecraft, and diplomatic arrangements to counterbalance the hegemon of the competitor.

A. Subramanyam Raju in his paper *India's Maritime Security: Some Observations,* brings to the fore the significance of Indian Ocean to India's security and analyses India's policy towards maritime security. Most of the maritime threats have transnational dimensions and it is essential for India to have greater cooperation with neighbours on maritime security. This paper examines the imperative of co-operation in joint naval patrolling, controlling of smuggling and pirate activities, strengthening of communication networks, institutionalization of economic co-operation in the exploration of sea resources, and concern for maritime issues faced by the littoral states of the Indian Ocean that are essential to establish and promote transnational, maritime and co-operative mechanisms to mitigate maritime security concerns.

We take this opportunity to place on record our deep sense of gratitude and appreciation to all the contributors for their scholarly papers and suggestions to the compendium. Our thanks are also due to New Century Publications, New Delhi, for taking up the publication of this book.

Thiruvananthapuram

Josukutty C.A.
J. Prabhash

1

Theoretical Foundations of India's Foreign Policy

M.J. Vinod

The paper strives to identify various modes, premises and arguments germane to a theoretical understanding of contemporary Indian foreign policy. To find an appropriate theoretical framework for the study of Indian foreign policy is an onerous task. India as the world's largest democracy with one-sixth of humanity and as the world's third largest economy is a given reality. Every country witnesses elements of continuity and change, following the change of governments. The issue is, how much of this continuity and change is there in Narendra Modi's foreign policy in relation to his predecessors. Some analysts emphasize that Indian foreign policy is distinguished by a new lexicon and imagery. There are five areas of the emerging change: the centrality given to economic and technological development; the orientation of domestic and foreign policies toward this objective; the emphasis on national power including military power; and stress on soft power; and a reduction in self-imposed constraints on actions that other countries may construe as inimical to their interests. [1] There seems to be a clearer articulation of India's national interests. All these premises are however subject to debate and discussion. The parliamentary elections held in 2014 resulted in the BJP and its allies securing a historic mandate, which has raised some serious questions about the future directions of Indian's foreign policy:

1. Has the mandate provided Modi a free hand to reshape India's foreign policy without being weighed down by domestic pulls and pressures?

2. Has Modi been able to remove many of the structural hurdles/bottlenecks constraining India's foreign policy?
3. What type of pro-activism can one associate with Modi's foreign policy?
4. Will India convert its military might into regional and global political influence?
5. Has Modi transformed the historical narrative about Indian foreign policy from that of a flailing power to a rising global power in the international comity of nations?

To address some of these questions and more, this paper intends to look at the theoretical foundations/Schools of thought in contemporary India's foreign policy. The paper will focus on the following schools, viz:

1. Nehruvian School.
2. Neo-liberal School.
3. Hyper-realist School.
4. Regionalists.

Nehruvian School

The Nehruvians tend to favour the continuation of the status quo. The near consensus in Indian foreign policy for close to four decades was represented by the Nehruvian school. The Panchsheel policy and its emphasis on non-intervention are visible indicators. The Nehruvian perspective towards non-alignment was perhaps more pragmatic and less doctrinaire. Non-alignment constituted the prescription to deal with great powers of the time. It represented an approach of strategic preparedness and trust with diplomacy. As a liberal internationalist, perhaps it was a natural outcome innate in Nehru's outlook. Problems and challenges were bound to surface en route, both in terms of Cold War logistics and the regional dynamics. The onset of the Cold War did present Nehru with a variety of systemic constraints too. Nehru believed that this was the only 'honourable policy' for India to take. In a way, non-alignment was an extension of Nehru's personality.

The imperative of development and the paucity of resources consistently afflicted his thought process. The need to protect and cherish India's hard-fought independence was a major factor too. Hence, Nehru believed that peace was a prerequisite for development and non-alignment was a prerequisite for peace. [2] Non-alignment was a natural outcome of the times and circumstances in which Nehru lived. Nehru's participation in the Congress of Oppressed Nationalities in Brussels in 1927 was an expression of these developments. As S. Gopal argued, this conference was a major turning point in Nehru's outlook and vision. Whereas Nehru fully understood the drive-to-power inherent in imperialism, and later was to provide an analysis of the expansionary tendencies inherent in certain ideologies, he failed to understand the potential for conflict inherent in creating territorially based order in Asia. [3]

Where principles and norms are in conflict with national interest considerations, on certain occasions, Nehru opted for protecting the national interests. Two examples illustrate the point well. Despite India's foreign policymakers stressing the need for the peaceful settlement of disputes, Nehru chose to end Portugal's 500-year rule over the enclave of Goa by force. In 1961, notwithstanding India's enunciation of the principle of peaceful co-existence, Indian soldiers and tanks rolled into Goa. [4] Perhaps Nehru was left with no option under the circumstances. Perhaps it can be argued that there was also an element of realism in Nehruvian idealism.

The theoretical arguments extended by the Nehruvians include the following:

1. Violence is not inevitable and war is not a natural/inherent activity.
2. Wars as Nehru had observed are made in the '*minds of men*'. Hence, it is in the *minds of men that war has to be eliminated.*
3. War can be tackled by wise cooperative policies among states; communication between governments and people.

4. Nehruvians argue that greater the opportunities for dialogue, contacts and communications, lesser the possibility of misunderstandings, misperceptions.
5. International organisations and inter-state negotiations also matter—this helps to institutionalise communication and contact. This enhances the chances for stability, cooperation and peace.
6. India should have enough force to defend itself, but not to make others fearful.
7. Nehruvians base internal security on a secular, democratic and socialist order. Use of force to enforce internal order should be the last resort.
8. Nehruvians are basically classical internationalists and emphasise the importance of diplomacy and greater understanding. [5]

In the aftermath of Independence, Nehru dominated the foreign policy and security landscape of India. Indian foreign policy rested on ideas, norms and values. Nehru had aspired to play the role of a bridge builder in world politics. His foreign policy sought to undermine the domination of the imperial powers as a whole. Perhaps Nehru ought to have struck a better balance between India's material and moral power base. Girija Kumar Bajpai's essential claim was that the acquisition of material power would in no way eclipse India's moral pre-eminence. Like all political leaders, Nehru too, had his strengths and weaknesses.

However, to assess Nehru's contribution purely within a zero-sum idealist or realist framework could be an oversimplification. The meaning and significance of Nehru's vision has to be understood in terms of how he perceived particular issues vis-à-vis their intrinsic value, as ends in themselves and/or as ways-and-means to achieve something more tangible. The Nehruvian 'strategy' needs to be understood in relation to the timing of decision-making, the framing of the policy debates and the justifications he extended in relation to particular policy decisions taken by him. Needless to say, one has to critique some of the policy outcomes too. The overall sense at that point of time was that Nehru perhaps knew best about foreign policy. Traditional Indian foreign policy tended to suggest that India has been a defensive power.

Hyper-Realists/Hyper-Nationalists

The realists argue that the success or failure of a country's foreign policy depends upon how it understands and relates to the power dynamics in its various manifestations. Most Realists see international interactions as an expression of state capabilities and the distribution of these military capabilities reflected throughout the international system. Some dismiss the role of ideology in foreign policy making. Others, however, insist that political ideology does matter and helps explain variation in state foreign policy actions. It also depends on how power is wielded. Hans Morgenthau had once observed that "the prestige of a nation is its reputation for power". That reputation, the reflection of the reality of power in the mind of the observers, can be as important as the reality of power itself. India has made an arduous journey from Nehruvian idealism to hard realism to economically driven pragmatism. [6]

The hyper realists tend to support the idea of fortress India and militarism. They have drawn their ideological influence from a variety of sources like the writings of Kautilya, Machiavelli, Thucydides, Hobbes and Morgenthau. Kautilya's Arthashastra actually records India's strategic thinking. The Arthashastra is an ancient Indian treatise on statecraft, economic policy and military strategy. Much of it has to do with war and diplomacy. Kautilya served as the chief adviser of Chandragupta, the first Mauryan emperor. He was among the foremost political thinkers and strategists. It is an important eye-opener to India's strategic culture. Almost half the treatise discusses foreign policy and defence. The Arthashastra is rich in ideas, conceptions, methodologies and is an incisive treatise. In the realm of foreign policy, it offers useful insights to the King. Kautilya argues that an ideal king is one who possesses the highest qualities of leadership, intellect, energy and other personal attributes.

The hyper-realists advocate the need to build commensurate military strength—both conventional and nuclear—as a derivative of higher economic strength, and extract more out of the present military expenditure outlays. There is a strong emphasis on military modernisation, as a means of assertion of India's rising global power status. [7] The hyper realists argue that the Indian power elites had developed a suspicion about power politics. It came to acquire a pejorative implication among the Nehruvian power brokers in particular. Hence, the hyper-realists argue that the linkage between power and politics need to be well understood. George Tanham has argued that India had been on the 'strategic defensive' throughout its history and reluctant to assert itself.

The core arguments of the hyperrealists are the following:

1. That security comes from strength. The governing metaphor of the hyperrealists is 'threat' and 'counter threat'. States are doomed to balance of 'power', 'deterrence' and 'war'. Balance-of-power is the basis of the world order.
2. War is a constant possibility in an anarchical international system. Though it can be destructive, it is also the basis for 'security' and 'autonomy'. In other words, war is not an aberration, but a natural tendency of international relations. Hence, preparing for war is 'not warmongering'. Rather it is 'responsible' and 'wise statecraft'.
3. The best way to achieve peace and stability is through the accumulation of military power and the 'willingness' to use force. The political/military leadership cannot avoid planning for the coercive use of force. In this sense, offence is the best form of defence.
4. Hyper-realists also tend to have their misgivings about the role of institutions, laws, treaties and agreements. Hence, they argue that though communication is necessary, it is not sufficient.

5. Hence what matters in international relations is 'force/power' in the *service of national interest.* It is an indispensable instrument in international relations. States may have to accept that force may be necessary in maximizing/promoting the national interest. The rest is only an illusion.
6. They argue that while economics/trade is important, yet this should not blind one to the reality of balance-of-power politics. This can be best met through greater pragmatism. China's rise and its intended and unintended implications and consequences can be a test case of this point.

The issue is whether the developments in Indian foreign policy since 1991 can be explained purely within the realist framework. Achin Vanik argues that realism as the conventional and dominant framework for explaining foreign policy behaviour, tends to fetish the notion of national interest. He argues that the post-Cold War world has basically evolved into a hub-and-spokes arrangement, with the US at the hub and connected by separate spokes bilaterally to all the major powers, each of which is more concerned about developing and sustaining its relationships with the hub, than with moving seriously along the rim against the hub. Various powers are bandwagoning to a greater or lesser degree with the US rather than striving seriously to challenge it. [8]

From an overall perspective, the hyper-realists invert the relationship between military and economic power. No amount of communication and/or economic interaction and interdependence can transform the relationship. What matters is the 'balance of power' which helps to regulate the relationship.

Neo-Liberals, Liberal Globalists, New Globalists and Liberal Internationalism

The neo-liberals prefer India to become a global economic player. Since the nineties, the liberal internationalists have become increasingly prominent/visible in the Indian foreign policy/economic debates. The neo-liberal perspective welcomes the unfettered flow of capital, goods and people as the means to the kind of global prosperity that would make conflict redundant.

[9] The issue is to what extent liberal internationalist thinking among elites is changing Indian foreign and economic policy. The new globalists arguments are largely driven by the economic boom in the post-liberalisation India and post-Cold War 'power realignment'. They place greater importance on trade and diplomacy. A powerful economy is a necessary pre-requisite for gaining an influential voice in the world comity of nations.

The main arguments of the neo-liberals are the following:

1. States pursue not only military power, but also economic well-being—economic strength is the ultimate basis for military power. Military domination is one way of achieving one's ends; economic domination is another.
2. Economic power can be more effective than military power, given its 'capacity to innovate'—in a global economy that makes states and societies secure.
3. States cannot escape the *logic of interdependence*, which makes for more pragmatic policies. Hence, states need not only focus on war, but also on the need for 'trade', 'investment' and 'diffusion of technology' and 'flow of capital' in a world that is getting increasingly globalized.
4. Capitalism is perceived as a basis for development, growth and human emancipation.
5. In a scenario of complex interdependence/mutual gain, force can be ineffective, even unusable. For neo-liberals 'force' is an 'outmoded' and 'blunt instrument'.

The larger issue according to the neo-liberals is about the source of economic well-being. Neo-liberals contend that economic well-being can only emanate from free market policies, free trade and economic interactions. It is India's economic growth/modernisation and its integration with the globalised world economy that will be its greatest assets and strengths. The centrists are known to be pragmatic in terms of balancing of economic development and military expenditures. They favour a 'neo-realist' foreign policy consensus of engaging India's immediate neighbours, backed by economic and military strength.

Regionalists

The regionalist foreign policy thrust is on the immediate neighbourhood and internal issues. As Deepa Ollapally argues, 'this school of thought leads to economics being driven by politics, and not the other way around'. [10] It will be a Himalayan blunder to ignore the neighbours, both immediate and distant. Prime Minister Narendra Modi began his charm offensive by making his first official visit to Bhutan where he met King Jigme Namgyel Wangchuck. His invitation to the Heads of State/Government of the immediate neighbours for his swearing in ceremony was an indication of his thinking. In this context, the Narendra Modi government had sent two powerful signals:

1. The urgency to reboot India's ties with the neighbourhood; and
2. Modi's government has turned the 'Look East' policy to an 'Act East' policy. Perhaps this reflects the need for India to play a more active/involved role in the region. In this context, the concept of 'regional multilateralism' assumes significance.

Which school Narendra Modi's government will stress, will depend on a variety of factors and forces—both internal and external. Perhaps the days of Nehruvian idealism of non-intervention and non-alignment—the hall mark of India's foreign policy for the last sixty years—has been deemphasised, though Prime Minister Narendra Modi has not publicly repudiated non-alignment. Both the 'realistic parameters of non-alignment' as well as the 'demands for alignment' need to be assessed. However, merely articulating Indian foreign policy in the language of non-alignment versus alignment is not sufficient to come to grips with contemporary Indian foreign policy. With a monetarist heart and a realist mind, Narendra Modi tends to value global power projections, a West-wards tilt and regional prominence, while balancing free-market fruits with nationalist roots. [11] However, it is too early to talk of a Modi doctrine in Indian foreign policy.

Nuclear Weapons, Nuclear Policy and Deterrence: A Case Study of the Views of the Nehruvians, Neo-liberals and Hyper-realists

If one were to take the issue of nuclear weapons and nuclear policy as a case study, the three main schools have commonalities and differences from the following perspectives, viz.:

1. The utility of nuclear weapons.
2. India's relationship/equations with the non-proliferation regime.
3. The nature of the deterrent.
4. The feasibility/desirability of disarmament.

The Nehruvians according to Kanti Bajpai contend that nuclear weapons are required for India's security, as long as they cannot be abolished. This makes the Nehruvian political standpoint harder to grasp after nuclear weapons came to play a role in foreign policy. [12] The main arguments of the Nehruvians according to him are as follows:

1. Nuclear weapons are a matter of abomination but if others have it, then India should also have them for deterrence.
2. The non-proliferation regime is basically unequal and hegemonistic. Hence, they need to be resisted.
3. They argue that nuclear disarmament is desirable and feasible. Disarmament is desirable because nuclear weapons in the hands of a few can be discriminatory.

Hence, to abolish nuclear weapons, what is perhaps required is a phased, time bound action plan, like what Rajiv Gandhi had initiated in 1988. The plan envisaged a universal and legally binding commitment. Rajiv Gandhi in his June 8, 1988 address to the UN argued that eventually nuclear disarmament will also "depend upon progress in the reduction of conventional armaments and forces". [13] The Nehruvians contend that even nuclear weapons are meant to be used for defensive purposes. The 'No First Use' policy is perhaps the outcome of such a policy.

The neo-liberals take a pragmatic perspective and believe that nuclear weapons are necessary for the country's security.

However, the following arguments bring out the commonalities and differences between the Nehruvians and the hyperrealists:

1. On the credibility of the non-proliferation regime, the neo-liberals argue that India should reconsider its opposition to some of the key elements of the regime, especially in the light of the Pokharan tests of 1998.
2. Neo-liberals argue that India could cut a deal with the international community by agreeing to join the CTBT, the FMCT, MTCR, the Nuclear Suppliers Group and in return demand de facto, if not de jure, recognition of its nuclear status.
3. Scepticism about disarmament varies among neo-liberals. Some are swayed by the Nehruvian perspective on the issue.

The hyper-realist arguments are on expected lines:

1. Nuclear weapons are primarily for deterrence. Hence, nuclear weapons have a political dimension/role.
2. Nuclear weapons are critical/fundamental to India's status as a rising power.
3. They argue that India should not join the non-proliferation regime as it is discriminatory. Moreover, India would need to continue testing, and for this, more fissile materials are necessary.
4. On the nature of the deterrent, hyper-realists are 'maximalists' given their views on nature of the threat, force size and structure, command and control, nuclear readiness and the logic of deterrence.

Kanti Bajpai argues that the Nehruvians, neo-liberals and the hyper-realists agree that India needs nuclear weapons for deterrence. In this sense, nuclear weapons are not just a military but also a political equaliser. The argument here is that nuclear weapons are also required in the diplomatic sense. However, they tend to have divergent views on the non-proliferation regime and on disarmament. Perhaps the neo-liberals will be more inclined to sign the CTBT.

In short, the Nehruvians and the neo-liberals take a more

minimalist position vis-à-vis the hyper-realists who opt for a more maximalist stance on the issue.

Conclusion

Narendra Modi's foreign policy seems to be driven by the following drivers:

1. To unburden Indian foreign policy from the ideological fixation of the Nehruvian times, without rejecting Nehru's legacy.
2. Restructuring and reorienting the foreign policy in keeping with the demands/pressures in the rapidly changing geo-politics of the Asia-Pacific region in particular.
3. Modi's foreign policy is also clearly driven by 'geo-economics'. Hence, trade will be the cornerstone of his foreign policy.

Narendra Modi seems to be redefining the terms on which India is likely to engage the region and the world. Certain sophistication seems to have gone into Modi's external affairs. Foreign Secretary Jaishankar articulates a proactive foreign policy as being based on a clear sense of its priorities, an integrated view of regions, and a more vigorous effort directed at confidently pursuing multiple relationships simultaneously and making a global impact. [14] It seems like he has no time for the rhetoric on non-alignment. The issue is whether this represents a move from personalised foreign policy to institutionalised foreign policy. [15] Modi's foreign policy reflects a mix of 'nationalist-led geo-politics' and 'expedient geo-economics'. This could help bridge the gap between the development aspirations/goals of the country and its foreign policy. Modi seems to have positioned himself as a pragmatic technocrat—focusing on reviving India's stagnant economy, dealing with the challenges posed by corruption, national security etc. In its approach and thinking, Indian foreign policy increasingly reflects an embrace of *realpolitik pragmatism.*

Perhaps Modi's foreign policy tends to reflect greater adeptness in terms of balance-of-power politics. These power dynamics are constantly happening whether India recognizes it or not. Normative principles will continue to be important in shaping thc world order. The core principles of Indian foreign policy will be the following: peace, development, justice and development, which is necessary for an equitable world order.

There are points of intersection between these various schools. Hence, almost all of them would for example, have reservations about India signing arms control agreements; they would oppose India joining any formal military alliance; suspicions/fears about China's role in the region and beyond remain; most of the schools oppose the use of force in international affairs etc. The ideas of these schools continue to be debated among policy makers, academics, technocrats, armed forces, media, intelligence agencies and think tanks. Perhaps, it is not proper to categorise the debate into pro- and anti-Nehruvian camps. Though Nehruvianism does not presently rule the strategic landscape, yet the scenario can be best categorised as Nehruvian and post-Nehruvian. The latter has to be understood factoring in the different government policies, leadership styles, issues, policies, debates, perceptions and misperceptions.

It is not in India's interest to lapse into pure Nehruvian idealism and also be caught in the 'dangerous hyper-realism'. In terms of India's ties with its neighbours, especially China and Pakistan, we see the predominance of the Nehruvian-neo-liberal schools, with bouts of hyper-realism. This is reflected in the series of summit meets, confidence building measures, trade, border negotiations etc. This has been accompanied simultaneously by tensions, differences and even war mongering. The cycle continues. Mark Twain had once observed that "history does not repeat itself, but it does rhyme".

Hence, there has been an element of continuity with change along with the historic opportunity for Narendra Modi to realign India's foreign policy priorities and goals. The tensions between altruism and national interests will continue to play out in India's foreign policy. Clearly, Indian foreign policy has become more argumentative and assertive in recent times.

Endnotes

1. http://www.thehindu.com/opinion/op-ed/comment-recalibrating-indias-foreign-policy/article6553306.ece?ref=relatedNews.
2. Raju, G. and C. Thomas (1979), "Non-alignment and Indian Security: Nehru's Rationale and Legacy", *Journal of Strategic Studies,* 2:2, 158.
3. Pratap Bhanu Mehta (2009), "Still under Nehru Shadow? The Absence of Foreign Policy Frameworks in India", *Indian Review,* 8:3, July-September, 209-233.
4. Hussein Solomon (2012), "Critical Reflections of Indian Foreign Policy: Between Kautilya and Ashoka", *South African Journal of International Affairs,* 19:1, 65-78.
5. Kanti Bajpai (2012), "India and the World", in Niraja Gopal and Pratap Bhanu Mehta (eds.), 'The Oxford Companion of Politics in India', Oxford, New Delhi, 521-541.
6. Rohan Mukherjee and David Malone (2011), "Indian Foreign Policy and Security Challenges", *International Affairs,* January Vol. 87, Issue 1, 87-104.
7. Kanti Bajpai (2013), "Does India do Grand Strategy", *Global Brief,* March 5.
8. http://www.india-seminar.com/2008/581/581_achin_vanaik.htm.
9. Pramit Pal Chaudhuri, available at: https://www.aspeninstitute.it/aspenia-online/article/india-superpower-or-subcontinent.
10. Deepa Ollapally (2010), "Understanding Foreign Policy Drivers in Rising India", Observer Research Foundation, January 6.
11. Anubhav Roy, available at: http://www.e-ir.info/2015/10/26/the-thatcherization-of-indias-foreign-policy.
12. Harriet Oliasen, available at: http://fokusindia.no/2012/10/why-nehruvianism-is-a-blast-from-the-past.
13. http://disarmingconflict.ca/2011/09/09/reviving-rajiv-gandhi%E2%80%99s-action-plan-for-nuclear-disarmament.
14. Prashanth Parmeshwaran, available at: http://thediplomat.com/2015/07/is-india-advancing-a-new-proactive-foreign-policy-under-modi.
15. Harsh V. Pant (2014), "Out with Non-Alignment, In with Modi Doctrine", *The Diplomat,* November 14.

2

India's Foreign Policy and Strategic Autonomy

Monish Tourangbam

The concept of strategic autonomy has been a guiding star in the evolution of independent India's foreign policy. Even as a newly independent country facing daunting internal and external challenges, India attempted to define its own path in manoeuvring international affairs, more complicated by the advent of the Cold War between the United States and the Soviet Union. India's decision not to join either of the two blocs brought its fair share of trials in terms of balancing its ties with the United States and the Soviet Union or their allies. With the end of the Cold War and the onset of India's economic liberalisation, India has opened its doors to Western countries, more specifically the United States in ways unthinkable during the Cold War. Today, as the spectre of a rising China becomes ubiquitous across the spectrum leading to security concerns, accruing out of the possibility of a rising hegemony in the eastern hemisphere, India and the United States or for that matter, America's allies like Japan and Australia sharing similar concerns are engaging in ways hitherto unseen.

India is undergoing a transition of its identity, from being seen as a "voice of the voiceless" to aspiring great power status, which takes into account the perceptions of other countries, especially other major powers as to where India stands in the international system. As such, the changing trajectory of India's foreign policy in the 21st century and the debates over the relevance and significance of strategic autonomy in India's strategy needs to be soberly and critically analysed. More than often, Western scholars and practitioners have accused India of being a naysayer when it comes to taking up responsibilities in the international system. Hence, it becomes imperative to analyse the prevailing views regarding India's role and potential for distribution of public goods and at the same time, critically assess India's view of its position in international affairs.

Breaking Foreign Policy Inertia

India's foreign policy strategy needs to be reflective of the changes in India's power potential and its changing ambitions and aspirations. The national interest primarily determines the foreign policy decision-making of any country. However, the changing capabilities also influence the nature of the interest of any country and the toolkit available to the country to achieve the objectives enshrined. As debates and deliberations abound regarding the contours of India's foreign policy in the 21st century, there is more continuity and changes that are there, are more incremental in nature, attempting to adequately take cognizance of the changes at home and abroad.

Operational changes are easy to see and recognize, but the undercurrent of the strategies in India's approach to the world and the changing nature of pivotal relationships may not be readily recognizable and at time recognized but not acknowledged. For instance, since the blossoming of the India-US relationship and the envisioning of the emerging strategic partnership, the two countries have conducted an unprecedented number of joint military exercises and defence trade has grown substantially. However, this reality is yet to translate into a macro understanding of what the two countries exactly want from the partnership, and fears of India falling into America's alliance trap still pervades in large sections of the political and the bureaucratic class.

When taboos of foreign policy are broken and new grounds are cleared for harvesting new relationships, inertias of internal and external behaviours impose constraints that take time to address. In more ways than one, foreign policy is also about reinventing traditional approaches to suit the emerging geo-political and geo-economic context. Thus, numerous analyses have attempted to make sense of the path of Indian foreign policy orientations. Will refurbishing the concept of non-alignment serve the interest of the country? If non-alignment conjures up images of Cold War alliances and the politics that eschewed; will the underlying concept of strategic autonomy better reflect India's new foreign policy strategy into the 21st century? As India embarks on the path of global recognition of its changing capabilities and ambitions, the push and pull of the old and the new influences in decision-making is apparent.

The China Factor

The changing phase of Indian diplomacy in the post-Cold War era has been largely determined by its economic rise and the linkages it has developed with the global market. Economic growth has led to a gradual transition from mere ideational greatness to search for material greatness, with a greater voice at the international high table. However, India's economic growth has taken place under the shadow of a bigger success story in neighbouring People's Republic of China. The economic rise of China and its strategic implications is perhaps the most singularly significant factor that has changed the way one looks at international affairs in recent times. China's rise has led to web of interlocking economies not only within Asia, but across the globe, visibly putting into effect the literal sense of interstate interdependence.

Though India lags behind China in almost all parameters of growth indicators, it will not be wrong to say that the concurrent rise of India and China has brought forth the debates around Asia-Pacific and the emerging geo-political construct of the Indo-Pacific. However, India shares a difficult relationship with China, and the shadow of India's military defeat at the hands of China in 1962 War looms large over Indian psyche, and surveys have shown that Indians in general look at China as a threat. One can change friends but not neighbours. And hence, the rise of an economic and military power like China breathing down its neck has significantly impacted the fashioning of Indian foreign policy.

Simultaneous with the economic rise of China has been an effort by the Chinese government to project a 'peaceful rise of China' to the rest of the world. It has invested in diplomatic efforts to project its rise as being commensurate with the peace and stability of the international system. It wants to be seen as working towards the internal development of the country and its people with no negative repercussions for the region and beyond. However, the rise of China has affected its strategic behaviour in a way that has invariably increased the threat perception of its neighbours, particularly among Southeast Asian countries that want a more engaged India in efforts to constrain the rise of a unilateral power in the region. In that pursuit, convergence can be found in India's 'Act East policy' and American's rebalancing strategy that attempts to maintain regional stability (Andersen and Verma, 2015: 97).

According to the Pew Research Centre that surveyed '*How Asians View Each Other*' in its 2014 report titled 'Global Opposition to U.S. Surveillance and Drones, but Limited Harm to America's Image: Many in Asia Worry about Conflict with China', only 30 percent of Chinese view India favourably, while 31 percent of Indians view China favourably, 72 percent of Indians are concerned about territorial disputes with China. Asians' concerns about China reflect the fact that, as Asia's largest economic and military power sitting at the centre of the region, Beijing has territorial disputes with many of its neighbours. There is widespread concern among public in East, Southeast and South Asia that these frictions could lead to military conflict (Pew Research Centre, 2014).

India: A Responsible Realist

Even as carpers in India's strategic community continue to see eminent vulnerabilities and challenges to India's independent decision-making while building ties with the US, this relationship has undoubtedly changed the trajectory of India's foreign policy. India's relationship with the US has given a new dimension to India's understanding of its own rising capabilities and aspirations amidst the changing distribution of capabilities, both regionally and globally. In essence, because of India's changing equations with the US, the notion of strategic autonomy better reflects the realities of world politics, and comes minus the anti-Western edge often identified with non-alignment. This understanding of strategic autonomy will be germane in navigating India's foreign policy priorities. Adding to the challenges of developing a more plural, open, and inclusive security architecture in the Asia-Pacific are the persistent strategic rivalries and protracted territorial and maritime disputes in the region, including the one between India and China. Besides trade and commerce that augments cooperative behaviour in the region, simultaneous increase in military spending among Asian countries, accentuate the security dilemma in the region (Tourangbam, 2014).

The increasing geo-political salience that the Indian Ocean region occupies and the increasing ambitions of the Chinese Navy in the region necessitate an adroit display of internal and external balancing from India's side. India's serious intent to build concrete ties with countries like Japan, Australia and the United States lend more currency to the strategic confluence of the Indian and the Pacific Oceans, augmenting the significance of the emerging Indo-Pacific region. The root for this convergence lay in these countries' strategic consonance to ensure stability of the Indo-Pacific trade corridors. India's Prime Minister Narendra Modi rightly pointed during his visit to Australia in July 2015, "...the world sees Australia to be at the heart of the Asia-Pacific and Indian Ocean region. This dynamic region holds the key to this world's future; and Australia is at its cross-currents. And, as Australia has become more engaged in this part of the world, we welcome its growing role in driving this region's prosperity and shaping its security" (Modi, 2014).

Likewise, the Tokyo Declaration for India-Japan Special Strategic and Global Partnership released during Prime Minister Modi's visit to Japan in September 2014 contended that a "a closer and stronger strategic partnership between India and Japan" was "indispensable for a prosperous future for the two countries and for advancing peace, stability and prosperity in the world, in particular, in the inter-connected Asia, Pacific and Indian Ocean Regions" (Ministry of External Affairs, 2014). The progress in the official trilateral dialogue between India, Japan and the United States was acknowledged. Both sides expressed hope that the trilateral understanding "would lead to concrete and demonstrable projects to advance their shared interests and that of other partners" (Ibid). Modi's successive visits to the three Indian Ocean nations of Seychelles, Mauritius and Sri Lanka have also accentuated the level of importance accorded to this emerging geo-political region.

China's strategic priorities in the Indian Ocean region has been a matter of debate across the world, and its ambitious advocacy of the 21st century Maritime Silk Road (MSR) commensurate with Chinese investments in port developments in South Asia has been a cause of concern for India. In a clear reflection of how smaller countries are playing their balancing act, the Sri Lankan Foreign Minister Mangala Samaraweera during his visit to Beijing in February 2015 said that Colombo was "...trying to ensure that there is a level playing field for all investors and a conducive environment for investment, based on the restoration of the rule of law, democracy, good governance and transparency" (Blanchard, 2015).

This testifies to the imperative for India to not only recognise the strategic autonomy of smaller countries but also manage their approach adroitly to prevent from harming India's interest. Emerging powers in Asia like India and extra-regional powers like the United States are reflecting the repercussions of China's rise in their strategic documents. *Non-alignment 2.0* in India's case has clearly discussed the complex relationship with a rising power like China in its vicinity. "China will, for the foreseeable future, remain a significant foreign policy and security challenge for India. It is one major power which impinges directly on India's geo-political space.

As its economic and military capabilities expand, its power differential with India is likely to widen", the strategic documents pointed out (Khilnani et al., 2012: 13). The geo-political as well as the geo-economic spaces of India and China, criss-crosses each other, necessitating sober analyses from both sides regarding the feasibility of finding more convergences in the relationship. There are increasing debates on whether China really sees India as a threat. However, there seems to be larger acknowledgement that India's intentions to partner with other countries in the region and beyond to manage China's rise are being watched keenly in Beijing. *Non-Alignment 2.0* contended:

"The retention of strong US maritime deployments in the Asia-Pacific theatre, a more proactive and assertive Japanese naval force projection, and a build-up of the naval capabilities of such key littoral states as Indonesia, Australia and Vietnam: all may help delay, if not deter, the projection of Chinese naval power in the Indian Ocean. We need to use this window of opportunity to build up our own naval capabilities" (Ibid).

Moreover, India is also wary that China's relatively increasing power vis-à-vis the US could lead to the US accommodating China to the detriment of India's interests. Thus, a more astute handling of relations is required where India's strategic partnerships with regional and extra-regional countries are augmented to enable a more transparent and stable Asia to grow. One of India's prominent analysts C. Rajamohan rightly argued that "protesting against the role of great powers in the region" was futile. "India needs a more purposeful policy to build on its natural geographic advantages in the subcontinent, deepen economic integration, promote regional connectivity, and resolve outstanding bilateral political disputes...The challenge for India is no longer about preventing the world from impinging on its choices, but to using its growing economic and political weight to shape the external environment to its benefit", he emphasised (Rajamohan, 2015: 30-31).

Adroit Diplomacy in a Multilateral Order

The complexities that Indian policymakers and leaders of India have to traverse in the increasingly globalised world, with intertwining economies and persisting strategic concerns is amply reflected in the contours of India-China relations. Prime Minister Modi's first visit to China generated enthusiastic crowds and attention from Indian and Chinese leaders, policymakers and media. The external manifestations of India's economic growth have accentuated the primacy attached to its economic engagements with the rest of the world. In China as well, Modi carried his 'Make in India' campaign that aims to turn India into a manufacturing hub.

Besides the overall continuity in India's foreign policy orientations, if a certain characterisation had to be identified that has set the new Prime Minister Modi led government apart, it has been the emphasis given to economic diplomacy in India's engagements with the rest of the world, whether it is with the immediate neighbourhood, extended neighbourhood or with the major powers of the world. India's outward looking liberalised economy is undergoing further reforms, setting its sights to playing a central role in agenda setting and decision-making in global financial matters. India intends to tweak the global financial architecture and maximize its gains through neo-liberal inter-country economic cooperation.

Prime Minister Modi has clearly intensified his 'Make in India' campaign and his advocacy of the three Ds: democracy, demand and demography as India's trump card. All of these efforts are directed at energizing the economics of India's foreign policy. His official travels ranging from smaller countries in the South Asian region to major powers of the international system is aimed towards recognising the interdependent nature of the international system and a belief that the practice of strategic autonomy best serves India's national interest.

As India chooses to embark on a benign projection of its rising power, it has become imperative to chart a foreign policy commensurate with its ambitions in Asia and the world, and demands augmentation of its fungible economic strength to increase its strategic influence. With great powers, comes great responsibilities, and India is at a great juncture in its history, travelling an upward journey to major power status. Clearly, Indian policymakers should create such a scenario where India's arrival as a major power in the international system should not be seen as a liability but as an asset. And upgrading its economic diplomacy, through efforts to making India a favoured destination for business and investment is a good way to go ahead.

A sound economic base at home and uninterrupted growth would lend more weight to India's ability to pursue its interests in the emerging multilateral global order. India's bargaining toolkit will be greatly strengthened in the process, paving the road to more pragmatic approaches to realise its goals in multilateral negotiations. Moreover, India will gain more traction to help determine the shape of things to come in the world, rather than be at the receiving end of rules made by others. India's increasing heft in the international system is reflected in the institutional roles that it plays in groups like the G20 and BRICS, especially post the global financial crisis, when the efficacy of the existing institutions is under scrutiny.

Analysts have argued that India has experienced "growth through participation in the multilateral order, and its development strategy and energy requirements make it dependent on stable globalization". According to them, India has growing economic, trade and energy stakes in literally every corner of the globe. Much of the trade and energy flows via the Indian Ocean, where India is an established maritime player but also faces enormous new demands and challenges. At this stage in its history, India has critical interests in just about every major multilateral regime and vital interests in several emerging regimes. The boundaries between Indian self-interest and the contours of the multilateral order have blurred. In short, India might have no choice but to influence the evolving multilateral order if it is to sustain its own interests (Sidhu et al., 2013: 3).

India's Foreign Secretary S. Jaishankar rightly argued during a lecture in Singapore: "In so far as larger international politics is concerned, India welcomes the growing reality of a multi-polar world, as it does, of a multi-polar Asia. We, therefore, want to build our bilateral relationships with all major players, confident that progress in one account opens up possibilities in others...You would have already noted more energetic diplomacy that seeks a larger and deeper footprint in the world, supported by soft-power initiatives like the International Day of Yoga. The transition in India is an expression of greater self-confidence. *Its foreign policy dimension is to aspire to be a leading power, rather than just a balancing power*" [empahsis added] (Jaishankar, 2015).

New Mandate and India's Worldview

The hopes pinned on India's new Prime Minister Narendra Modi who came to power with a huge mandate and his emphasis on reenergizing India's growth curve has certainly lent a new lease of life to the Indian diplomacy. The new vigour found in India's foreign policy approach perhaps gives an opportunity to steer India's vision for regional and global prominence, and fine tune the implementation of such a vision (Andersen and Verma, 2015). Symbolism is a critical component of foreign policy practice and Modi has showed easy camaraderie with global orders. There is a personal and informal touch injected into the formalities of diplomacy. Chintamani Mahaptra, Professor at the School of International Studies, Jawaharlal Nehru University, argued:

"Modi's style of diplomacy has been marked by the symbolism of a deep personal rapport with foreign leaders.

Since the role of the individual in foreign policy implementation of any country is crucial, importance of Modi addressing foreign leaders with their first names, expressing friendship with bear hugs, taking selfies, breaking protocols to meet them outside the capitals, feeding the fishes, *chai pe charcha* etc. should not be belittled. History is witness to the fact that good policies in foreign affairs do not get implemented in time without the attention of the leaders at the top of the decision-making structure, and several bilateral standoffs are relatively quickly resolved when the heads of Governments respond. Thus, rapport between leaders is essential and Modi has taken extra pains to develop such affinity with world leaders" (Mahapatra, 2015).

This was clearly exemplified, among many, in the way the Chinese President Xi Jinping received Prime Minister Modi at his hometown Xian, in response to Modi hosting him at his home state of Gujarat. The gesture was aimed not only to inject a new life into the relationship but also to highlight the importance of other regions and provinces, besides New Delhi and Beijing. Not only are New Delhi and the various departments under the government interfacing with their counterparts in other countries, but also state governments have become increasingly important in India's engagement with other countries.

The rapport that he was able to develop with President Barack Obama and pulling off a sort of coup de grace with Obama attending India's Republic Day Celebrations was a notable achievement in the annals of India-US diplomatic history. Modi drew vast support and welcome from the Indian Diaspora in the United States. His speech at the Madison Square Garden, managed to overwhelm Indians not only present in the stadium but all around the world, with various new proposals and mechanisms announced to largely ease people-to-people ties between the two countries.

The publishing of a joint op-ed in The Washington Post titled, 'A Renewed US-India Partnership for the 21st Century' by

PM Modi and President Obama, was a bold statement made by both the leaders in delivering a message of how serious and committed they were in taking the relationship forward. More than with any other country, it is India's relationship with the United States that has really tested the practice of strategic autonomy in India's foreign policy approach. One of the stumbling blocks to the developing India-US strategic partnership is the recurrence of perceptions that look at India as a reluctant partner, and the US as an unreliable power. More than often, India going closer to the US is seen as a recipe for India's squandering of its strategic autonomy, which is unfortunate. Such an approach shows India's lack of confidence in its rising power capabilities that present with it, an opportunity to control its own sail (Tourangbam, 2015: 126).

Consistency in the trajectory of the relationship is something that both India and the US are yet to achieve. There have been periods of marked improvement in the relationship which have been suddenly punctuated by periods of heightened dismay and mistrust. The pursuit of a more substantial strategic partnership between the two countries is still ongoing. However, in the last decade, India-US relations has developed to the extent of being called the 'defining partnership of the 21st century' and entered a phase of maturity where tactical missteps cannot overwhelm the emerging strategic partnership. While many carpers of the relationship still seem to discount it as detrimental to India's strategic interest, India's growing engagement with the US should also be seen as a practice of strategic autonomy.

Strategic autonomy is not anathema to strategic engagements. The rise of India's capabilities and aspirations in Asia, and at the global level, are in the interest of the US; and the sustenance of US power and influence in Asia, and globally, are in the interest of India (Council on Foreign Relations and Aspen Institute India, 2011). The Joint Strategic Vision for the Asia-Pacific and Indian Ocean Region has clearly affirmed "the importance of safeguarding maritime security and ensuring freedom of navigation and over flight throughout the region, especially in the South China Sea" (The White House, 2015).

This view was also reflected during Nisha Desai Biswal's, Assistant Secretary, Bureau of South and Central Asian Affairs, testimony before the House Foreign Affairs Committee, Subcommittee on Asia and the Pacific on July 24, 2014. India's rise, according to her, "as a regional and global power, and its economic and strategic growth, are deeply in the US interest". "Like the United States, India increasingly sees its future in a secure, connected, and prosperous Asia Pacific. We not only share democratic values but also a deep interest in a peaceful and rules-based order...We see a partnership with India that spans east, west, north, and south to advance our shared interests across the Indo-Pacific region", she argued (Biswal, 2014).

If for India, the US is important as a global power that could substantially help push up India's influence globally, as it did with the signing of the civilian nuclear agreement and helping India gain the Nuclear Suppliers Group (NSG) waiver, India is equally important for the furtherance of US foreign policy objectives in the Asia-Pacific region. India could be what some call the "bridge state" in the changing global order. The document *Non-Alignment 2.0* has pointed out:

"The structures of competition in the global system will present India with a range of partnership choices. For a start, India will be sought after in great power competition. This presents a great historical opportunity for India. This diverse identity and the multiple interests that it underpins are actually our greatest strategic assets at the global level. For it means, that India can be a unique bridge between different worlds. Indeed, India's bridging potential is one we must leverage and turn to our active benefit" (Khilnani et al., 31) [sic].

India's economic rise has had significant dividends across the spectrum, and a realist orientation of its foreign policy approach is imminent. With increasing capabilities, India's own conception of its goals and objectives will be surely, even if gradually, reoriented. The dynamics of India's worldview and other's perception of emerging India is highly consequential for the future directions of India's foreign policy. India's engagement with major powers needs a nuanced examination of what India needs from them and what India can give them. India's ability for independent decision-making will depend on augmentation of its all-round capabilities and clearer vision of what it aspires that necessitates a more pragmatic appreciation of its national interest.

The triangular relationship between India, China and the United States will reflect India's ability to manoeuvre great power politics amid India's own ambition to be a great power. There may be issues where India might find it more prudent to go along with China and others where a partnership with the United States might be of greater consequence. For instance, on many sectors of the economic front, India-China relationship could go forward while India and the United States might share more conducive interests on the security front (Rajamohan, 2015:110-111). However, the push and pulls of geo-politics are seldom linear and India should be proactive in sensing the situation and preparing for the worst as well as for the best of times. Mahapatra precisely argued, "...While no foreign policy vision document or a white paper or strategy report has been issued by the new Government, the directions of Indian foreign policy appear to have a clear-cut target and that is to make India an important global player individually where necessary, bilaterally where required, and multilaterally where relevant" (Mahapatra, 2015).

Conclusion

In a rapidly globalising world in which the gravity of power is shifting from the West to the East, India stands at the cusp of both opportunities and challenges. The economic dynamism of Asia has been accentuating the interdependent nature of the international system putting a premium on the benefits of cooperation and coordination. The rise of China followed by India's emergence as a power to reckon with has been the cover story of the 21st century. The increasing salience that Asia-Pacific has got in America's strategic lexicon and the emphasis being put on the new geo-political construct of Indo-Pacific is symptomatic of the changes in the undercurrents of the international system. In recent times, there have been marked changes in terms of India's perception of its own standing in international affairs and in how the world looks at the changes in India.

Hence, both the identity and image of India is undergoing a significant transition, where it needs to efficiently manage the projection of its power capabilities to be seen as an asset and not a liability to the future of a stable regional and global order. As India, reflective of its civilisational glory, aspires to invoke its identity as a *vishwaguru* (a teacher for the world), it also needs to focus on the importance of domestic growth with social and economic inclusiveness. India is traversing a complicated geo-political landscape where strategic rivalries exist simultaneously with interlinking trade and commerce. As India develops newer understandings of its power capabilities, it needs to emerge with a responsible realist emphasis in its foreign policy approach that discards any anti-Western fixation. The holy grail of India's approach in international relations should be of national interest and reflective of its changing power capabilities.

In that pursuit, there should be better appreciation of the need for injection of effective manpower into the foreign policymaking mechanism and re-energise the process of building internal consensus on India's national interest. A pragmatic interpretation of the concept of strategic autonomy is required that takes into account its relevance in the context of the 21st century and calls for simultaneous management of relations with multiple power centres of the international system. The practice of strategic autonomy in the emerging world order would be highly strengthened by a foreign policy approach that is in sync with uninterrupted internal development in India.

References

Andersen, Walter and Shrey Verma (2015), "Washington's India

Pivot: Is It Compatible with Modi's Asian Ambitions?", *India Quarterly*, 71(2): 95-109.

Biswal, Nisha Desai (2014), "U.S.-India Relations under the Modi Government", The House Foreign Affairs Committee, Subcommittee on Asia and the Pacific, Washington, DC, July 24, 2014, available at: http://www.state.gov/p/sca/rls/rmks/2014/229739.htm.

Blanchard, Ben (2015), "Sri Lanka Says China to be Consulted on any Project Re-think", *Reuters*, February 27, 2015, available at: http://in.reuters.com/article/2015/02/27/china-sri-lanka-idINKBN0LV0KW20150227.

Council on Foreign Relations and Aspen Institute India (2011), "The United States and India: A Shared Strategic Future", available at: file:///C:/Users/Acer/Downloads/USIndia_jointstudygroup_IIGG.pdf.

Jaishankar, S. (2015), "IISS Fullerton Lecture by Foreign Secretary in Singapore", Ministry of External Affairs, Government of India, July 20, 2015, available at: http://mea.gov.in/Speeches-Statements.htm?dtl/25493/IISS_Fullerton_Lecture_by_Foreign_Secretary_in_Singapore.

Khilnani, Sunil et al. (2012), "Non-Alignment 2.0: A Foreign and Strategic Policy for India in the Twenty First Century", available at: http://www.cprindia.org/sites/default/files/NonAlignment%202.0_1.pdf.

Mahapatra, Chintamani (2015), "Modi 365: Reshaping India's Foreign Policy", *The Pioneer*, May 31, 2015, available at: http://www.dailypioneer.com/sunday-edition/agenda/cover-story/modi-365-reshaping-indias-foreign-policy.html.

Ministry of External Affairs (2014), "Tokyo Declaration for India: Japan's Special Strategic and Global Partnership", September 1, 2014, available at: http://mea.gov.in/bilateral-documents.htm?dtl/23965/Tokyo_Declaration_for_India__Japan_Special_Strategic_and_Global_Partnership.

Modi, Narendra (2014), "Prime Minister's Address to the Joint Session of the Australian Parliament", Ministry of External Affairs, Government of India, November 18, 2014, available at:

http://mea.gov.in/outoging-visit-detail.htm?24269/Prime+Ministers+Address+to+the+Joint+Session+of+the+Australian+Parliament+18+November+2014.

Pew Research Centre (2014), "How Asians View Each Other", in 'Global Opposition to U.S. Surveillance and Drones, but Limited Harm to America's Image', available at: http://www.pewglobal.org/2014/07/14/chapter-4-how-asians-view-each-other.

Rajamohan, C. (2015), "Modi's World: Expanding India's Sphere of Influence", Harper Collins, New Delhi.

Sidhu, Waheguru Pal Singh, et al. (2013), "A Hesitant Rule Shaper", in Waheguru Pal Singh Sidhu, et al. (ed.) 'Shaping the Emerging World: India and the Multilateral Order', Foundation, Books, New Delhi.

The White House (2015), "U.S.-India Joint Strategic Vision for the Asia-Pacific and Indian Ocean Region", Office of the Press Secretary, January 25, 2015, available at: https://www.whitehouse.gov/the-press-office/2015/01/25/us-india-joint-strategic-vision-asia-pacific-and-indian-ocean-region.

Tourangbam, Monish (2014), "Indo-Pacific and the Practice of Strategic Autonomy," *Indian Foreign Affairs Journal*, debate on 'Indo-Pacific: An Emerging Geopolitical Construct—India's Interests, Stakes and Challenges', April-June, 9(2):115-120.

—-(2015), "Indo-US Strategic Partnership: Who's Afraid of an Alliance?", *Indian Foreign Affairs Journal,* debate on Indo-U.S. Strategic Partnership: Current Trends and Expectations, April-June, 10(2): 126-132.

3

India and the Changing Contexts of Deterrence

W. Lawrence S. Prabhakar

The concept and the theories of deterrence constitute a pivotal construct upon which national security strategies are constructed. Deterrence elucidates the capacity to impact violence on the adversary or another state. It is a dominant motivating factor in influencing the adversary or another state's behaviour (Schelling, 1966). Deterrence theory entails the use of rational choice and game-centric models arguing that deterrence success is more likely if the defending state's credibility of its attacking potential against its adversary is high. Rational Deterrence theory is the central paradigm that elucidates the concept and operations of deterrence. It is based on military balance, signalling and bargaining power, reputations for resolve and interests at stake (Huth, 1999).

In the context of India's national security policy and in terms of its evolution and contexts, the role of deterrence plays a pivotal role in the determination of its national security strategy. India's conceptions of deterrence have been in much debate since Independence as it configured its national security policy. Broadly speaking, deterrence has always bordered on deterrence by denial and deterrence by punishment as the dichotomous entity that determines the posture and operations of deterrence (Rajagopolan, 2010).

Through the wars of 1948, 1962, 1965, 1971 and 1999 India's deterrence posture had undergone substantial transformation (Basrur, 2009). The two nuclear tests of 1974 and 1998 had reinforced the nuclear deterrence posture of India with the elucidation of a credible minimum nuclear deterrence in place with an assured retaliatory capability. There had been considerable debate on India's 'Nuclear No First Use' policy and the debate continues.

India's contexts of deterrence however has to be viewed, contextualized and analysed from the perspectives of a multi-tier threat perceptions that could be in four stages. Stage I is the threat of terrorist or asymmetric attacks on India and the imperative for India to calibrate its asymmetric deterrence at the sub-conventional level vis-à-vis asymmetric actors that are operating with or without external state support. Stage II would deal with the initiation of limited war with the effect to pursue conventional war operations in one or all sectors vis-à-vis asymmetric actors with state support. Stage III envisages full scope conventional war against a state adversary and the pursuit of objectives that would entail conventional war operations with conventional deterrence in place. Stage IV would be the escalation to the resort of nuclear weapons, if and when the adversary attacks India with nuclear weapons with a first strike. Deliberating the four-stage escalation process of India's deterrence is pivotal to the understanding of India's national security imperatives and the operational contexts of India's deterrence.

The presentation would endeavour to: (a) locate the contexts of India's vistas of deterrence; (b) elucidate the substantive concerns of India's vistas of deterrence; and (c) analyse the escalatory contexts of India's conceptions of deterrence.

Deterrence theory entails the use of rational choice and game-centric models arguing that deterrence success is more likely if the defending state's credibility of its attacking potential against its adversary is high. Rational Deterrence theory is the central paradigm that elucidates the concept and operations of deterrence. The operational contexts of deterrence are based on military balance, signalling and bargaining power, reputations for resolve and interests at stake (Lebow and Stein, 1989).

Deterrence theory and operations pre-supposes to deal with state actors characterised by mutuality of interests and rationality of actions bound by value systems that are recognised by states as unitary actors. Deterrence rests on the certitude of assured destruction and the credibility of retaliation to a first strike. The operational criteria of deterrence are uniformly the same despite the size and complexity of the arsenals.

The pivot of India's security and its foreign policy rests on the resilience of India's deterrence. India's deterrence constitutes the grand strategic as well as the operational milieu of its security strategy. India had always advertised that its scope of deterrence posture is minimalist. But the definition of minimalism has not been defined. In the discussion on India's deterrence, there could be the typologies in terms of its conventional deterrence, deterrence vis-à-vis asymmetric threats and challenges, deterrence vis-à-vis strategic nuclear threats and deterrence vis-à-vis other WMD threats. India's pivotal strength and resilience had been its conventional deterrence that had been its mainstay vis-à-vis Pakistan since 1947 and China and continues till date.

The Indian Nuclear Doctrine of August 1999 was subsequently operationalised in January 2003 and elucidates the aspects of credibility, survivability, assured retaliation, no-first-use, command and control systems etc. India's deterrence however, interplays between its conventional and nuclear dimensions. It synergizes with each other. Southern Asia also features the triangularity of nuclear deterrence between India-China-Pakistan that is unique in the post-Cold War era. The triangular formation of deterrence is actually a combination of two complex relationships of nuclear dyads between India and China, India and Pakistan and a convergent relationship between China and Pakistan. In terms of the structural aspects of deterrence, Southern Asia features an asymmetry of power between India, China and Pakistan and also features the asymmetry of conventional capabilities between the three states.

This could be in the context of the deployment and the evidence of the asymmetry of nuclear forces, the asymmetry of intentions of the three powers and the asymmetry of nuclear doctrines among them. The second debate about nuclear deterrence in Southern Asia is that between the 'nuclear optimists' vs. 'nuclear pessimists' (Feaver, 1995).

The nuclear optimists are those who favour the balance of power among the emerging nuclear powers and are positive in terms of horizontal expansion of nuclear powers and their capabilities, while the nuclear pessimists do argue about the proliferation consequences of both horizontal and vertical proliferation of nuclear weapons. Southern Asia's deterrence is marked by the horizontal and vertical proliferation that is stable and instable between India and Pakistan. The third fact is that the nuclear deterrence of the region is also influenced by extra-regional nuclear presence and regional deterrence featuring the US military's nuclear presence in the Southern Asia-Indian Ocean and its role in influencing India and Pakistan nuclear balance. China's extended deterrence in Southern Asia *inter alia* Pakistan is the reality that provides an extended nuclear deterrence to Pakistan.

India's Vistas of Deterrence

India's nuclear doctrine and posture is based on the concept of nuclear minimalism that believes in maintaining a nuclear force posture based on an effective retaliatory capability. India's nuclear arsenal is not arithmetically calibrated but built on the need to develop effective targeting strategy for a retaliatory strike against Pakistan and China and for contingencies beyond its current threat assessment. In principle, India accepts a defensive-defence approach of a nuclear no-first use that would imply its reliance on conventional defences with its nuclear forces for deterrence (Prabhakar, 2002).

India's minimal nuclear deterrence faces two several critical challenges. The first is a symmetrical conventional challenge in the Southern Asian region where India's minimal nuclear deterrence posture faces a rapidly modernizing Chinese nuclear arsenal that is larger in size and diversified in capabilities along with the critical challenge of a first-strike

Pakistani arsenal that is increasingly vulnerable to extreme political elements, capable of internal destabilization.

The second is an asymmetrical challenge of the increasing destabilization of Pakistan and the prospect of the fall of nuclear weapons in the hands of terrorist groups based and operating from Pakistan. In an age of asymmetric conflicts, wars between two nuclear powers would always start from the initiation of low intensity conflicts by terrorist groups escalating to levels of preventive war, limited war, and limited war with nuclear strikes, culminating into a full-fledged conventional war running the full-scale escalatory ladder (Basrur, 2009a).

India's minimum nuclear deterrence (MND) is structured on the following operational criteria:

Targeting of Retaliation: India's minimal nuclear posture affects its scope of targeting strategy. India's targeting strategy is constrained by the factors of: (i) size of India's arsenal, (ii) the yield of its weapons, (iii) the nature of satellite-based intelligence of targets, and (iv) the accuracy of the means of delivery.

India's minimal nuclear arsenal has to focus on *counterforce targeting* (striking nuclear forces, launch control centres, weapon storage sites, field formations, troops concentrations, air and naval bases, logistics, and repair and supply facilities) requiring accurate and timely means of delivery with sufficient range. Given the reality of Pakistan and China as the two-front nuclear threat, India obviously faces a wide range of its targets struck and also has to retaliate in a second-third strike cycle (Tellis, 2001).

Given the single-warhead missiles and manned aircraft, there would be challenges in the penetration of dense air defences in the counterforce targeting of Chinese assets. Besides, China has excellent protective and dispersal means of its missiles in highly mobile configurations and hardened silos in mountain caves. India, would thus have to, resort to more counter value targeting of industrial, economic, and population centres which require less accuracy nuclear weapons. With regards to Pakistan, India expects a much larger first strike in response to its conventional escalation arising from Pakistani provocations.

India's posture and response is for an uncontrolled escalation by seeking the capability to destroy as much of Pakistan's nuclear deterrent as possible as a "damage limitation" targeting strategy.

Choice of Retaliation is the second critical operational criterion for India's minimal nuclear deterrence and posture. Is it going to be proportionate and graduated retaliation or massive retaliation? Minimal deterrence suggests retaliation in a similar quantum. An optimal minimal deterrence would seek to seize the initiative and to terminate aggression on India's terms. In that case, India must possess survivable nuclear retaliatory forces and the command and control to execute a massive retaliatory strike which, in turn, requires the capacity to transform India's dispersed de-alerted force into a coherent strike force on short notice.

The means to resort to a coordinated response by India to a joint Pakistani and Chinese attack is increasingly crucial. This worst-case scenario is not considered likely, but nonetheless demands a serious review. India's minimal nuclear deterrence however has the fateful choice of confronting a larger Chinese attack across the spectrum of targets that strains India's inventory of nuclear weapons and the means of delivery.

The importance of India's pursuit of a triad of nuclear delivery means is thus very crucial with a larger segment of India's nuclear warheads that should be deployed in fleet ballistic submarines and cruise missile submarines which provides India, stealth, dispersal and assured retaliatory capability on a variety of Chinese and Pakistani targets thus reinforcing its minimal nuclear deterrence. However, this is going to be a prolonged development in terms of the numbers of platforms and long ranges of missiles to target China.

Certainty of Retaliation is the third operational criterion on which the credibility of the Indian nuclear deterrent hinges. The certain means of retaliation is more important than the speed with which retaliation would be made. Certain retaliation can be assured only by the survivability and dispersal of India's nuclear assets. Given the prospect of strong first strike by Pakistan and a Chinese coordinated attack, the scale of destruction of India's nuclear and infrastructure assets would be massive. Minimal nuclear deterrence should convey the signal of certainty of unacceptable damage to the aggressors as a means to reinforce deterrence.

Augmentation of Retaliation would require the transformation of India's 'force-in-being' nuclear arsenal to be converted into a strike force and launched in the aftermath of first strikes by Pakistan and China or respond to a Chinese supporting strike in a second-third strike cycles. The extent of delay before retaliation would be determined by how India manages its nuclear "day after". There would be a delay in retaliation as the political leadership configures to the responses and more importantly the post-disaster management to organize the riposte. What would be important is the augmentation of capabilities for retaliation; would it be symbolic and limited, or a massive response that would destroy the aggressor's society beyond repair?

Whatever nuclear capabilities India pursues, its command and control arrangements need to be reinforced to ensure the credibility of its deterrence. And whatever be the scenario, India requires a robust system for the early warning of nuclear attacks. There must be a high degree of mobility for India's nuclear assets—delivery systems, warheads, dummies, and decoys—and proper linkage to the National Command Authority, the apex command and control structure along with alternate, survivable national command posts that connect national leaders, civilian members of the atomic establishment, and leaders of the armed forces to direct retaliatory strike operations.

Four issues dominate the debate of what constitutes the benchmarks for the future of India's nuclear arsenal and how its adequacy would be vital to maintain nuclear deterrence in an age that is characterized by rapid strides of strategic modernization:

1. The existing and emergent size of India's fissile material

stocks that is insulated for weapons production is vital for the preservation, maintenance and renewal of its arsenal. It is quite likely that India would have to face the prospect of a new era that calls for deep cuts in nuclear arms with stiff non-proliferation regimes like the fissile material cut-off treaty and reinforcement of comprehensive test ban. India's international nuclear engagement should not infringe on its strategic autonomy or its ability to sustain fissile material stocks, sufficient to maintain its minimal nuclear deterrence.

2. China's nuclear modernization and its shift of nuclear posture for sufficient defence aiming for a maximalist capability is evident in its new JL-2 SLBMs and the DF-21 IRBMs and the DF-31, DF-41 ICBMs, which critically affects India. India's imperative is to maintain a robust and sufficient nuclear force posture for its retaliatory targeting capability of China that should be in enhanced yield and range of delivery. Minimal nuclear deterrence does not limit India in terms of yield of nuclear weapons nor does it limit to number of nuclear weapons; the important issue is the adequacy of the number of weapons, weapon ranges and yield that are critical.
3. The China-Pakistan collusion and the two-theatre adversarial nuclear-missile posture that India would have to contend in the coming years is a serious challenge. India would have to inevitably face a nuclear dual jeopardy of any conflict escalation. It would be naïve on the part of any political-strategic dispensation in India to compartmentalize and hyphenate the conflict in the region. Pakistan's nuclear arsenal is absolutely a Chinese arsenal, buttressed by China's extended deterrence. Notwithstanding all the positives of good relations with China, India contends a strategic geography that inevitably brings in China in any escalation of conflict with Pakistan.
4. The rapidly changing international strategic environment characterizes the nuclear modernization and deployment of

space-based offensive strike assets that aid the nuclear arms race between the United States, China and Russia and it has its full impact on India. With Chinese strategic modernization in its nuclear and space arsenals in full momentum, there is a sustained cascading impact on India's force posture. The US and Russian modernization and upgradation efforts has its impact on China which in turn sustains its initiatives.

Notwithstanding all the rhetoric of nuclear disarmament, the spate of global strategic modernization would have a powerful unequivocal impact on India's minimal nuclear deterrence. India's nuclear deterrence posture is defensive-defence with certitudes of assured retaliation premised on minimum credible deterrence and active defence in the imminence of threats and aggression. India's sources of doctrine and conduct are based on the civilian control of the military and nuclear forces; the policy and higher direction of strategy are controlled by the political elite and the bureaucratic elite; the escalation dynamics based on active defence and retaliatory actions with potential for significant escalation dominance of conventional retaliation preferring a crisis termination by diplomatic and political means derived from a position of sufficient conventional strength. Thus, for India, nuclear weapons are for deterrence rather than war-fighting with a no-first use practice in place. However, a credible no-first use should be backed by substantial retaliatory second strike capabilities. In India's case, this is growing and is modest at present.

India's nuclear doctrine has several contradictions and confusions—is it a deliberate ambiguity or an inadvertent confusion?

India's deterrence posture seeks a diplomatic and political means of conflict termination derived from a position of sufficient conventional strength.

In the operational realm, India faces a superior nuclear-conventional adversary China. India has very modest real targeting of China's homeland while China's land-based and sea-based missiles target India. China's extended deterrence covers Pakistan and it sets the premise for a triangular deterrence between India-China-Pakistan.

In the realm of asymmetric threats and deterrence, India contends a growing spectrum of asymmetric threats from Pakistan and the stakes are raised for a sub-conventional war that would be the initial triggers. Asymmetric threats and sub-conventional wars like the Kargil War of 1999 and the Mumbai 26/11 attacks have tested the resilience of the Indian conventional deterrence—India had to fight the sub-conventional wars with the Pakistani provocation to the maximalist levels. The Kargil War of 1999 was the test that Pakistan exploited—the sub-conventional space in its war fighting with the nuclear backdrop. In the face of Pakistan's nuclear adventurism, India has been preparing for a swift conventional retribution in the face of the asymmetric attacks and threats by the development of the "Cold Start" doctrine that would effectively neutral the Pakistani asymmetric attacks and also stave off the prospect of a possible Pakistani first use of nuclear weapons. Pakistan in retaliation has developed the HATF-IX NASR tactical nuclear missile that would target Indian rapid deployment formations effectively by responding to India's Cold Start.

On the other hand, China's nuclear doctrine has shifted from *Minimum Deterrence* to *Limited Deterrence*—emphasizing on: (a) active defence to minimise potential damage; (b) offensive strike to take 'war to the enemy'; and (c) tactical nuclear war operational plans for local war contingencies. China's deterrence postures vis-à-vis India has been in the following categories (Saalman, 2012):

1. Traditional: recessed, denial, minimum, limited.
2. Conceptual: regional, offensive regional, containment.
3. Operational: punishment, invasion, maritime.

The India-China deterrence order is stable as both countries affirm no-first-use with respect to each other (although there are debates to revise the NFU by both India and China). India and China have been engaged in beefing up of conventional deterrence through a spate of conventional forces modernization.

India has a well-negotiated military and nuclear confidence building measures with that assuages fears of resorting to nuclear escalation.

Issues and Challenges in India's Deterrence Posture

India's nuclear doctrine and its deterrence posture are essentially premised on "minimalism" and its preference to a no-first-use and "non-use" against non-nuclear weapon states. India's credible nuclear deterrence thus ought to serve the following objectives:

1. Sufficient and survivable nuclear forces both in terms of warheads and means of delivery able to inflict unacceptable damage.
2. Nuclear forces must be operationally prepared at all times.
3. Effective intelligence and early warning capabilities.
4. A robust command and control system.
5. Will to employ nuclear forces.
6. Communication of deterrence capability.

Certain challenges are evident in India's deterrence position:

1. India's credible minimum deterrent may not be one that fits the size vis-à-vis Pakistan and China; since China has been expanding its nuclear arsenal. This has to be viewed in the context of the increasing numbers of Pakistan's nuclear arsenal and their assured missile targeting along with China.
2. India's nuclear forces are no longer de-mated and disassembled since India's long range missiles like *Agni* and the SLBM solid-fuelled are encapsulated and thus the nuclear warhead is premated with the missile in its canisterized form; it is possible that other systems are in de-mated stage.

3. India's NFU pledge is eroded when the question of India being attacked by chemical and biological weapons is there. India's retaliation in that context would be by nuclear weapons (which is according to the 2003 version of the Nuclear Doctrine). Secondly, India's conventional targeting of Pakistan's nuclear assets could actually lead to nuclear explosion thus leading Pakistan to use it rather than loose it. India's NFU pledge would thus hold more during peace time with ambiguities during crisis or hostilities period.
4. India's nuclear deterrence and doctrine is silent on the issue of non-state actors and their role in a possible crisis escalation. Certain factors are relevant in this discussion:

- Non-state actors that are backed by adversarial state with *intents and capabilities* to target India with WMD viz. chemical, biological or radiological weapons or devices—which warrants India to modify its NFU to target the non-state entities also (Kulkarni and Sinha, 2012).
- Non-state actors that are transnational in character and pertain to regions rather than particular states—this factor makes India's nuclear deterrence inapplicable since deterrence is applied to states and not to groups. Nuclear deterrence relies on the clear and categorical identification of the adversary—India in this case would have to resort to coercive diplomacy that would have costs for India and India would be reluctant.
- Non-state actors succeeding in acquiring or inventing nuclear weapons (radiological dispersal devices) and targeting India? India's nuclear deterrence would find it extremely difficult since: (a) non-state actors cannot be deterred because they are free of obligations that come with the legitimacy of being recognised players in the international system; (b) Non-state actors cannot be identified territorially, thus the idea of retaliatory attack gives way—invulnerable to the credibility of retaliatory measures thus undermines deterrence as a strategy; (c)

non-state actors do not share the same value-systems and world-views as the Indian state—hence the role of rationality in deterrence is ruled out while deterring violent non-state actors (Kulkarni and Tanvi, 2012).

Crisis Escalation and Deterrence

Crisis escalation and deterrence are tenacious constructs in the history and path of deterrence history of India and Pakistan. Crisis and deterrence had seen the two phases of the pre-nuclear and the post-nuclear phases in the pathways of India-Pakistan relations.

The India-Pakistan crisis threshold is identified from its past crisis by the following thresholds. Stage I is the threat of terrorist or asymmetric attacks on India and the imperative for India to calibrate its asymmetric deterrence at the sub-conventional level vis-à-vis asymmetric actors that are operating with or without external state support (Shaun, 2011). Stage II would deal with the initiation of limited war with the effect to pursue conventional war operations in one or all sectors vis-à-vis asymmetric actors with state support. Stage III envisages full scope conventional war against a state adversary and the pursuit of objectives that would entail conventional war operations with conventional deterrence in place. Stage IV would be the escalation to the resort of nuclear weapons, if and when the adversary attacks India with nuclear weapons with a first strike.

The crisis escalation ladder between India and Pakistan is compounded by the prospect of introduction of tactical nuclear weapons by Pakistan at the level of initiation of the conflict. India's 'Cold Start Doctrine' envisages for the rapid use of India's superior conventional forces in the repulse and the counterattack of Pakistan's forces that have abetted the non-state actors in the asymmetric and sub-conventional war against India. 'Cold Start' also envisages the targeting of Pakistani battlefield nuclear assets by conventional strike, pre-empting their use, thus attempting to negate the possible

Pakistani use of tactical nuclear weapons.

Pakistani response has been the deployment of the HATF-IX NASR surface to surface nuclear tipped missile on advancing Indian formations that would cripple the Indian conventional forces assault on Pakistan and thus it lowers the threshold of nuclear use to battlefield nuclear weapons by Pakistan, prompting Indian nuclear retaliation.

The resilience of India's conventional deterrence is thus challenged by the introduction of Pakistani tactical nuclear weapons that would complicate any retaliation by India from unprovoked attack by Pakistan-based asymmetric groups.

In summation, it is evident that India's deterrence had gradually shifted from conventional to nuclear and to the asymmetric as the loci of threats and challenges has changed from conventional war to asymmetric conflict in the backdrop of nuclear weapons in the subcontinent. India's deterrence with China has remained stable, with both sides elucidating the NFU and the rough terms of the conventional balance. New targeting strategies and modernization of strategic platforms, however has implications for India as China moves to limited deterrence with sufficiency. One of the predominant factors that is influencing deterrence is the defence transformation of conventional forces and enhanced conventional deterrence that India is employing aimed at bolstering its deterrence posture. Tactical nuclear weapons and their possible deployment by China and Pakistan lowers the deterrence threshold for India and thus erodes India's conventional strengths and contributes to escalatory options.

References

Basrur, Rajesh (2009), "Minimum Deterrence and India's Nuclear Security", Stanford University Press, Stanford, Palo Alto.

Basrur, Rajesh M. (2009a), "The Lessons of Kargil as Learned by India", in Peter R. Lavoy (ed.), 'Asymmetric Warfare in South Asia: The Causes and Consequences of the Kargil Conflict', Cambridge University Press.

Feaver, Peter, D. (1995), "Optimists, Pessimists, and Theories of

Nuclear Proliferation Management: A Debate", *Security Studies,* Volume 4, Issue 4.

Gregory, Shaun (2011), "Terrorist Tactics in Pakistan Threaten Nuclear Weapons Safety", *CTC Sentinel*, June 1, 2011, available at:
http://bit.ly/lVsRgW.

Huth, Paul (1999), "Deterrence and International Conflict: Empirical Findings and Theoretical Debates", *Annual Review of Political Science*, June, 25-48.

Kulkarni, Tanvi and Sinha, Alankrita (2012), "Undermining Deterrence: The Non-State Actors and India's Nuclear Doctrine".

Kulkarni, Tanvi (2012), "Debate: India's Nuclear Doctrine and Radiological Weapons", IPCS Article # 3576, February 16, 2012, Institute of Peace and Conflict Studies, New Delhi, available at:
http://bit.ly/JSXGkV.

Lebow, Richard N. and Stein, Janice (1989), "Rational Deterrence Theory: I think, Therefore I Deter", *World Politics*, Volume 41, Issue 2, January.

Prabhakar, Lawrence W. (2002), "The Challenge of Minimal Nuclear Deterrence", in Michael Krepon (ed.), 'Nuclear Risk Reduction in South Asia', The Henry Stimson Centre, Washington.

Rajagopalan, Rajesh (2010), "India's Nuclear Policy and Major Powers' Nuclear Policies and International Order in the Twenty-first Century", National Institute for Defence Studies, International Symposium on Security Affairs.

Saalman, Lora (2012), "The China-India Nuclear Crossroads: China, India, and the New Paradigm", Carnegie Endowment for International Peace, Washington DC.

Schelling, Thomas C. (1966), "The Strategy of Conflict", Harvard University Press, Cambridge, MA.

Tellis, Ashley (2001), "India's Emerging Nuclear Posture: Between Recessed Deterrent and Ready Arsenal", RAND, Santa Monica.

4

India's Nuclear Strategy: An Analysis

Suratha Kumar Malik

The Backdrop: From Nuclear Estrangement to Co-operation

The Indian peaceful nuclear test of 1974 made Western nations conscious of the existing loopholes in the non-proliferation regime and heightened their 'atomic dilemma'. It was alleged that India diverted the nuclear technologies intended for civilian purposes under the Canada-India-Reactor-US (CIRUS) agreement with Canada and the US. Thus, post-1974, India was regarded as a 'nuclear pariah'. [1] The US Congress passed the Nuclear Non-Proliferation Act of 1978 (NNPA), which barred nuclear exports unless the non-nuclear weapon state accepted comprehensive International Atomic Energy Agency (IAEA) safeguards. India was internationally isolated, yet it refused to accede to the NPT and pursued an ambiguous policy on nuclear weapons.

In 1998, India conducted a series of nuclear weapons explosions and declared it a nuclear weapon state. The then US president, Bill Clinton, immediately retorted that the 'Indian government had put itself at odds with the international community' as well as 'at the wrong side of history'. [2] In the aftermath of the 1998 nuclear tests, the Clinton administration imposed sanctions as per the Glenn Amendment, thereby restricting bilateral and multilateral economic assistance. [3] In addition, the non-statutory measures also curtailed high-level visits and military-to-military contacts.

Nonetheless, within seven years of the 1998 nuclear tests, in an extreme policy reversal, the successive George W. Bush administration offered nuclear cooperation to India. On July 18,

2005, US President George Bush and the Indian Prime Minister, Manmohan Singh, issued a joint declaration envisaging full civil nuclear cooperation. Significantly, the US declared India 'a responsible state with advanced nuclear technology'. The declaration included path-breaking pledges on both sides. [4] The US committed, *inter alia*, to: (i) offer civilian nuclear technologies to alleviate Indian concerns regarding energy security; (ii) seek to adjust US laws and policies in order to realize the goals of nuclear cooperation; and (iii) encourage its [supplier] friends to alter existing international regimes in order to enable civil nuclear cooperation with India.

In reciprocation, India committed itself to: (i) segregate its civilian and military facilities and place its civilian facilities under IAEA safeguards; (ii) honour the voluntary moratorium on nuclear testing; (iii) sign and adhere to an IAEA additional protocol with respect to civilian nuclear facilities; (iv) refrain from transfer of enrichment and reprocessing technologies to states that do not have them and support international efforts to limit their spread; and (v) strengthen its export controls through comprehensive national legislation to curb proliferation of sensitive technologies and harmonize them as per Missile Technology Control Regime (MTCR) and Nuclear Suppliers Group (NSG) guidelines. [5]

Based on the July 2005 joint declaration, during President Bush's March 2006 visit to India, the two sides finalized a plan for the separation of Indian civilian and military facilities. They also mutually agreed to 'limit the spread of enrichment and reprocessing technologies' and 'support the conclusion of a Fissile Material Cut-off Treaty'. Subsequently, on December 18, 2006, President Bush signed into law the Henry Hyde United States-India Peaceful Atomic Energy Cooperation Act (hereafter, the Henry Hyde Act). [6] Interestingly, it was passed with strong bipartisan support in the US Congress. The Henry Hyde Act was described as an 'enabling legislation' as it created legal space, hitherto blocked by the NNPA, for resuming nuclear trade with India—a non-signatory of the NPT and a *de facto* nuclear weapon state. Nonetheless, Congress did attach certain clauses to emphasize the non-proliferation measures: the President must annually certify that India is adhering to the terms of the agreement; and, most significantly, the deal will lapse if India conducts further nuclear tests. [7]

Based on the earlier agreements (July 2005 and March 2006) and the Henry Hyde legislation, a separate technical agreement, popularly called the Indo-US 123 agreement, was signed by the two countries. [8] It specified detailed responsibilities of, and conditions for, the two nations. There were certain requirements India needed to fulfil before the agreement could be operationalised—a safeguard agreement with the IAEA and approval from the NSG. On the fulfilment of the conditions by India, the 123 agreement was introduced in the US Congress and it passed with an overwhelming majority in both the House of Representatives and the Senate. Finally, the US-India Nuclear Cooperation Bill was signed into law by President Bush in December 2008. [9]

There was widespread consensus among scholars that the Bush administration's neo-realist objective of forging a strategic partnership with India vis-à-vis China was the primary determinant of this nuclear pact. [10] It was believed that Bush's strategy was to 'cultivate a partnership with India and enhance India's international power. A more powerful and collegial India will balance China's power in Asia'. [11]

The persistent US-India nuclear estrangement not only impinged on bilateral relations, but also kept the recalcitrant India outside the nuclear non-proliferation regime. On this account, scholars considered the nuclear rapprochement between the US and India to be a positive development. [12] Paul called it a 'radical initiative', as otherwise the nuclear estrangement between India and the US showed 'no signs of ending'. [13] Ashok Kapur argued that the agreement 'levelled the playing field in the sphere of nuclear negotiations between "nuclear haves" and "nuclear have-nots". [14]

Some intellectuals expressed concerns regarding the

implications of the deal for India's nuclear weapons programme. Arun Shourie thoroughly analyzed the terms of the US-India agreement and related US legislation, concluding that Washington desired that 'India [be] drained of its strategic nuclear programme, and thus [become] a dependent India'. [15] He warned that the US planned ultimately to 'rollback and eventually eliminate the nuclear weapons capability of India'. [16] Similarly, Bharat Karnad opined, 'this deal amounts to death by stagnation for the Indian nuclear weapons programme'. [17] He emphasized that for India to be treated as 'a country of consequence', it is important to have a thermonuclear deterrent—'the prime currency of power in the new millennium'. The US has significant 'test data from the 1,800 [sic] nuclear tests and a computing ability of 100 teraflops and a gigantic ICF (Inertial Confinement Fusion) facility to obtain miniature thermonuclear explosions; its belief that it can do without testing is well-founded'. [18]

Unlike the US, India cannot afford to give up the nuclear testing, as it has neither the data nor the technology to conduct simulated nuclear tests in order to develop a thermonuclear deterrent. In this context, R. Rajaraman pointed out that India only intended to build a minimum nuclear deterrent and a 'minimal deterrence force does not call for a boundless open-ended nuclear arsenal'. [19] Allaying the fears of the critics, he argued, 'There will be no effect on the strategic programme, there will be no deceleration in our three-stage nuclear power programme…and there will be no effect on our advanced R& D programme'. [20]

Response within India on Nuclear Issues

In the beginning of April 2014, Manmohan Singh was addressing a conference at the Institute for Defence Studies and Analyses (IDSA) titled, "A Nuclear Weapon-Free World: From Conception to Reality", where he casually urged the creation of a global convention to forswear the first use of nuclear weapons. Following Singh's remarks, the then opposition *Bharatiya Janata Party* (BJP) instantly issued a rejoinder in its election manifesto, stating that the party "believes that the strategic gains acquired by India during the [earlier BJP-led] Atal Behari Vajpayee regime on the nuclear programme have been frittered away by [Singh's] Congress. Hence, the BJP pledged to study in detail India's nuclear doctrine, and revise and update it, to make it relevant to [the] challenges of current times. BJP spokespeople clarified that a review of India's no-first-use policy would be accorded priority if the party came to power. Modi's campaigning for the 2014 election, subsequently declared that there would be "no compromise" on no first use, which reflected India's "cultural inheritance" (whatever that means).

India's no-first-use policy was originally declared by the BJP and the National Democratic Alliance government after it conducted the May 1998 nuclear tests. The prime minister at that time, Atal Behari Vajpayee, stated thereafter that India would pursue a policy of no first use of nuclear weapons vis-à-vis other nuclear-armed states and would not use these weapons against non-nuclear countries. This restraint was also embedded in the BJP's draft nuclear doctrine, declared in August 1999, which took several years to be finalized. It was finally endorsed by the Cabinet Committee on Security and officially promulgated in January 2003.

Consequently, India's no-first-use policy and its nuclear doctrine are BJP formulations. The Congress party adopted them and, with Singh's April speech, simply sought to extend no-first-use globally. This makes the BJP's concern with its own no-first-use policy and nuclear doctrine part of the mystery of Singh's proposal.

India's Nuclear Strategy: The Theoretical Debate

The past few years have produced considerable debate over India's nuclear strategy and posture. [21] Much of it has revolved around the credibility of India's nuclear arsenal [22] (Chari, 2014; Global Security Newswire, 2009; Joshi, 2014;

Koithara, 2012; Menon, 2014; O'Donnell and Pant, 2014; Rajaraman, 2014). This is an important question because it goes to the heart of India's capacity to deter its adversaries. Is the Indian deterrent properly organised? Are its capabilities enough? What makes a deterrent credible? The ongoing debate has produced three broad positions: that India's nuclear weapons are inadequate for deterrence; that they are sufficient to meet the requirements of minimum deterrence; and that weapons development is reaching for excessive capabilities. But to resolve such a debate, it is first necessary to know: how *does* deterrence work?

For all the differences aired, there is remarkably little or no disagreement on the meaning and fundamental requirements of minimum deterrence. Everyone seems to agree that the central principle of deterrence is "assured/secure second strike capability". From this, flows the criteria for assessing the effectiveness of an arsenal: the survivability, reliability and accuracy of weapons, plus an efficient system of command control. To deter, so it went (and still goes), one has to survive a first strike and be sure to retaliate sufficiently well to create large-scale damage.

Indian theorizing about the requirements of deterrence, drawing heavily from American strategic literature, rests almost entirely on an uncritical acceptance of this edifice. [23] It is time to take a closer look. The foundational concept of assured second strike capability and its derivatives emerged from a series of seminal writings that emanated from the American strategic establishment in the 1950s and 1960s, notably from the RAND Corporation [24] which better represents the intellectual bedrock of American nuclear doctrine and strategy of Albert Wohlstetter. His 1958 paper on the Delicate Balance of Terror—more widely disseminated in a *Foreign Affairs* article in 1959—presents the core precepts of deterrence as he saw them (Wohlstetter, 1958; Wohlstetter, 1959).

A set of ideas drawn from the writings of Patrick Blackett

(Blackett, 1961; Blackett, 1962) which offers a powerful critique of the notion that secure second strike capability is vital to the working of nuclear deterrence and provide a sound intellectual basis for a truly minimalist approach toward nuclear deterrence. [25] He was critical of Wohlstetter and provided an alternative basis for thinking about the requirements of nuclear deterrence which in effect rejected the notion that second strike capability is the *sine qua non* of successful nuclear deterrence. His debate with Wohlstetter is instructive because it draws attention to the roots of the question "how much is enough?" As will become evident, Blackett's analysis was more insightful than Wohlstetter's. Indian strategists would do well to consider Blackett's analysis with care. [26]

Ironically, policy circles were familiar with Blackett's views on nuclear weapons. Nehru appointed him defence advisor, in which capacity he produced a report on the organization of India's defence apparatus (Blackett, 1948). The report, which led to the establishment of the Defence Science Organization, later the Defence Research and Development Organisation (DRDO), was warmly received by Nehru (Letter, 1948). Blackett was also close to Homi Bhabha, often called the father of the Indian nuclear programme and a strong advocate of nuclear weapons for India, though Blackett himself had reservations about the value of nuclear weapons (Speech, 1974). Blackett's position on nuclear weapons finds an echo in contemporary India in numerous ways. He was a staunch campaigner for nuclear disarmament and an early advocate of no-first-use (Howard, 1985).

Blackett offered a systematic refutation of the conception of deterrence that was predominant in American universities and in think tanks like the RAND Corporation. [27] He was particularly severe on Wohlstetter, whose views on the requirements of deterrence crystallized into official doctrine and produced the central tenet of "secure second strike capability" that quickly became deeply embedded in most strategic thinking about nuclear weapons in the United States and later elsewhere (Blackett, 1961; Blackett, 1962; Wohlstetter, 1958; Wohlstetter, 1959). The chief points made by Blackett were as follows: [28]

First, one need not threaten to obliterate the opponent's society in order to deter. Second, a nuclear surprise attack that destroys much of one's arsenal is extremely unlikely to happen. Wohlstetter's reasoning was based on the American experience of Pearl Harbour, i.e. the possibility of catastrophic damage inflicted by a similar surprise attack. Third, Wohlstetter held that an attacker who struck first would have the advantage, which meant that the defender, in order to deter effectively, would have to: (a) absorb the strike and have enough forces to retaliate; and (b) ensure that surviving retaliatory forces would be sufficiently strong to cause the desired damage by means of a successful second strike. The clear inference was that relative quantities and quality matter a great deal: the nuclear balance is important in ensuring that one has sufficient survivable weapons. The overarching argument put forward by Blackett was that the choices before an aggressor state are stark: only if it is fully confident that there will be no retaliation can it takes the risk of striking first —and no one can be that certain.

Thus, deterrence rests ultimately not on the defender's certainty of hitting back after absorbing a first strike, but on the aggressor's *uncertainty of being able to avoid retaliation.* Even if the two sides are numerically unequal in the size and capabilities of their nuclear arsenals, a "stronger" power cannot risk the possibility of retaliation by a "weaker" one because it cannot know in advance the level of retaliation that it may have to face. In short, most arguments about assured second strike capability are not in tune with the reality faced by policy makers.

Limitations of Nuclear Deterrence

There are valid grounds to revisit India's nuclear doctrine, but on the conceptual front, the limitations of nuclear deterrence have become apparent. In important ways, India's acquisition of nuclear weapons has not increased its security. While nuclear weapons have obvious relevance for the external dimensions of national security, they cannot ameliorate threats to India's territorial integrity that arise from domestic discontent or from cross-border militancy and terrorism emanating from Pakistan. In other words, nuclear weapons cannot provide any defence against the sub-conventional threats to India's national security from extremist elements within its own territory or, especially, against those who receive moral and material assistance from across the border. As Singh repeatedly warned, the internal threats to India's national security are critical to its overall national security challenges. Nuclear weapons provide no defence against these dangers.

The evidence in this regard is overwhelming and discernible from continuing unrest in the state of Jammu and Kashmir and in North-east India and from Maoist violence in central and east India. In a larger sense, no doubt, nuclear deterrence permits peaceful conditions to be established, a situation that is conducive to economic progress and the stimulation of regional trade and commerce. However, an entire spectrum of security threats also arises, ranging from border incursions to sub-conventional warfare and cross-border terrorism and militancy. Nuclear weapons provide no security against this range of existential security threats.

Pakistan Ups the Ante

The establishment of nuclear deterrence vis-à-vis Pakistan had only limited value for India's overall national security. It did not deter Pakistan's cross-border incursions in winter of 1998 and spring of 1999 into the Kargil sector of Jammu and Kashmir, which led to a short but intense conflict ending in the ouster of Pakistan's regular and irregular forces. Yet despite India's overwhelming superiority in conventional arms, the effects of nuclear deterrence inhibited it from attacking Pakistan's lines of communications across the border or from enlarging the theatre of conflict along the border to relieve pressure on the beleaguered Kargil sector.

Significantly, these operations revealed that a nuclearized Pakistan had constrained New Delhi from launching a counter offensive elsewhere along the Line of Control or into Pakistan to relieve pressure on Indian forces in Kargil. New Delhi decided that it would exhibit restraint and not expand the theatre of conflict. Political considerations were said to be at play, as India wished to establish that it was a responsible nuclear power by not escalating the conflict. There was also a subliminal desire among Indian leaders to paint Pakistan into a corner by highlighting its irresponsible conduct in attacking across recognized borders without any provocation. There is little doubt, however, that this restraint was also informed by New Delhi's awareness that an escalation of this border conflict could become uncontrollable and leads inexorably toward the nuclear threshold.

Pakistan's decision to deploy tactical nuclear weapons in a battlefield mode along the India-Pakistan border can be surmised from a report by Hans M. Kristensen and Robert Norris of the Federation of American Scientists that identified Pakistan and China as either having or developing non-strategic nuclear weapons. Pakistan had made clear, Kristensen told the *Times of India*, that it was developing its nuclear-capable Nasr (or Hatf IX) missile for use against invading Indian troop formations that Pakistan does not have the conventional capabilities to defeat. These weapons, according to Indian experts, are meant to be used along the border in case of any skirmish with the Indian Army. The Nasr is described as a 60 kilometre [37 miles] ballistic missile launched from a mobile twin-canister launcher". According to Pakistan's Inter Services Public Relations, the Nasr also has "shoot and scoot attributes" to serve as a quick response system to add deterrence value to Pakistan's strategic weapons development programme at shorter ranges...to deter evolving threats.

These developments have highlighted the insufficiency of India's no-first-use policy to deter Pakistan's destabilizing strategy. For one thing, this policy articulation frees Pakistan of the uncertainty and angst that India might contemplate against the pre-emptive use of nuclear weapons to deal with terrorist attacks or limited conventional strikes by Pakistan. Pakistan could also go to the extent of deploying its short-range Nasr missile without being concerned that India would target it with its own nuclear missiles. For another, the determinism inherent in India's nuclear doctrine that any level of nuclear attack will invite massive retaliation is too extreme to gain much credibility. It defies logic to threaten an adversary with nuclear annihilation to deter or defend against a tactical nuclear strike on an advancing military formation.

Pakistan, for its part, has not countenanced a no-first-use policy on the grounds that the weaker conventionally armed power has to rely on nuclear weapons to ensure its security. However, conventional wisdom warns that deployment of nuclear weapons along the border makes these arms vulnerable to attack, which, in turn, could generate a "use or lose" mentality on the part of their possessor. Pakistan argues that locating tactical nuclear weapons along the India-Pakistan border in a state of battle-readiness enables it to counter India's Cold Start strategy, which envisages positioning offensive, battle-ready forces along the India-Pakistan border to deter any cross-border attack.

Pakistan claims that deploying its tactical nuclear weapons would provide it with 'full spectrum deterrence' against India. It is arguable that India's commitment to a no-first-use posture has encouraged Pakistan to adopt its present adventurist strategy, secure in the belief that it could undertake provocative actions without the angst that India might contemplate a nuclear riposte. Its provocative actions would include promoting cross-border militancy and terrorism into India and even brazen actions like the attack on the Indian Parliament in 2001 or the Mumbai attacks in 2008. Arguably, the adoption of a deliberately vague policy in regard to nuclear retaliation by India, instead of the certitude of a no-first-use declaration, might have better served India's overall strategic ends. Apart from that, the no-first-use policy, which has been incorporated into India's nuclear doctrine, has several other infirmities.

An Inadequate Doctrine

The decision by the Cabinet Committee on Security to endorse India's nuclear doctrine (1999) makes clear that India will use nuclear weapons only to retaliate against a nuclear attack on its territories or on Indian forces anywhere; that nuclear weapons will not be used against non-nuclear states; but that, in the event of a major attack by biological or chemical weapons, India retains the option of retaliating with nuclear weapons. This enumeration of India's qualified no-first-use policy doctrine is flawed on several counts.

First, it does not address the possibility of an attack by non-state actors, which is the present and imminent danger. And how would India address an attack by an international organization like Al-Qaeda that is situated in several countries in the proximity of India? Second, how would a "major attack" with biological or chemical weapons be identified? What is "major" and what is "minor" is debatable. This issue is significant since biological and chemical weapons are not truly weapons of mass *destruction*, but they are certainly weapons of mass *disruption*. Non-state actors might favour these weapons due to the comparative ease of their manufacture, concealment, and transportation. Third, serious difficulties arise in any attempt to identify the perpetrator of a biological or chemical weapons attack that could be undertaken by state or non-state actors or, not inconceivably, by a non-state actor assisted by a state actor. This issue is ultimately a question of reliable forensics, which is at a rudimentary stage of development. The difficulty in identifying those guilty of chemical weapon attacks in Syria is instructive here.

India's no-first-use declaration cannot be separated from the country's overall nuclear doctrine as it has been articulated since 1999. Inadequate as it is, this doctrine deserves to be reviewed in the light of changes over the past fifteen years. The current nuclear doctrine dictates that nuclear retaliation against a first strike would be "massive" and designed to inflict "unacceptable damage" upon the attacker. This is an unrealistic certitude because, ethically, punishing large numbers of non-combatants contravenes the laws of war. Besides, threatening massive retaliation against any level of nuclear attack, which would inevitably trigger assured nuclear annihilation in a binary adversarial situation, is hardly a credible option. No doubt, it raises a ticklish question: Would India then favour a counterforce strategy? India's stated adherence to an assured and massive second strike suggests the latter. The present doctrine fetishizes acquisition of a "credible minimum deterrent". But India is seeking a force structure that is no different from that established by the United States or the former Soviet Union. India seeks a strategic triad comprising land-based, airborne, and underwater nuclear weapon systems that will require increasing resources.

It is arguable whether India's strategic circumstances require a naval component for its deterrent or whether the country requires only a submarine-based deterrent, on the assumption that the nuclear deterrent posture ultimately rests on the survivability of the nuclear arsenal. Land- and air-based systems are more vulnerable to counterattack and destruction than submarine-based missiles are. That leads to the argument that taking the deterrent out to sea would ensure the acquisition of an invulnerable second strike capability. This question has not been seriously discussed in India, resulting in vociferous demands from the three services that the government concede some component of the nuclear deterrent to each of them.

Criticism is widespread that there is little transparency about the size and structure of India's nuclear forces and what its credible minimum deterrent comprises in terms of weapons systems. Instead of debating this issue, official spokesmen have argued that it is impossible to define what a credible minimum deterrent requires since there can be no "fixity" in this regard, which suggests that the contours of the credible minimum deterrent are a moving target. Incidentally, India's armed forces have been kept out of the nuclear decision-making process; hence, there is a touch of unreality about these declarations on nuclear force structures.

Conclusion and Suggestions

The entire calculus that underlies the central principle of deterrence orthodoxy—that "secure second strike capability" is vital for effective deterrence—lacks empirical grounding. All deterrence is, in this sense, minimum deterrence. Even a small risk of retaliation posed to a potential aggressor suffices to deter because it poses the risk of very high-level damage within a very short time frame—a calculus that challenges any potential political gain arising from war. Furthermore, one cannot have confidence in relying on controlled or "tactical" uses of nuclear weapons. The risk of escalation in the fog of war means that any crossing of the nuclear threshold can very quickly result in indiscriminate mass destruction. Logically, there is no need for deterrence to rest on assured retaliation or to worry overly about the "vulnerability" of one's forces. Indian policy makers and strategists need to rethink the intellectual foundations of nuclear deterrence. A number of critical points need to be contemplated with care.

- Serious consideration needs to be given to a more realistic doctrine that rests on the principles outlined by Blackett and confirmed by historical experience across the board. A study group comprising civilian and military experts should be appointed to articulate a truly minimalist doctrine of deterrence. The construction of an optimal minimum deterrence doctrine should be based on extensive debate over the ideas of minimalists like Blackett and General K. Sundarji as well as a careful scrutiny of strategic history.
- The contradiction between 'minimum deterrence' and

'maximum credible' should be overcome and what is that 'minimum' should be defined in terms of quantity and quality.

- The concept of "assured/secure second strike capability" may be discarded as it is empty of meaningful content. There is no evidence whatsoever that this principle actually works. Its primary function is to encourage the open-ended expansion of nuclear arsenals, which may benefit the sectional interests of specific organizations, but not national security interests. Even a powerful country like the US has no such principle like 'second strike' and it has the principle for 'first strike'. Does India have sufficient retaliation capacity to absorb the first strike and go for an assured second strike?
- The term *credible* should be dropped from the nomenclature of Indian deterrence doctrine. If states with less than 1 percent of the forces possessed by their rivals can exercise deterrence, then "credibility" is of doubtful strategic meaning. One has only to look at one's own perception of adversaries: do Indian decision makers worry very much about the credibility of their adversaries' weapons? This approach logically encourages minimalist perceptions of deterrence requirements.
- Careful consideration needs to be given to the numbers and types of weapons systems desirable for effective deterrence. Excessive augmentation of capabilities wastes resources that would be better utilized for other needs.
- Above all, it is time for civilian officials to obtain a better understanding of the requirements of nuclear deterrence. Political responsibility requires that civilian policy makers come to grips with the complexities of the nuclear revolution.

Endnotes

1. Kux, Dennis, "India and the United States: Estranged Democracies 1941-1991", National Defence University Press, Washington, DC, 199, p. 123.
2. CNN News, "Clinton Says India is on 'Wrong Side of History' with Nuclear Tests", May 16, 1998.

3. Chellaney, Brahma (1994), "Non-proliferation: An Indian Critique of US Export Controls", *Orbis*, 38(3), Summer, p. 44.
4. See, The Indo-U.S. Joint Statement, July 18, 2005, Washington, DC, available at: http://www.indianembassy.org/press_release/2005/July/21.htm.
5. Ibid.
6. Perkovich, George (2010), "Global Implications of the U.S.-India Deal", *Daedalus*, 139(1), Winter; Ashley J. Tellis, "What Should We Expect from India as a Strategic Partner", in Henry Sokolski (ed.), 'Gauging U.S.-Indian Strategic Cooperation', Strategic Studies Institute, Carlisle, PA, 2007, pp. 231-258; Mario E. Carranza, 'From Non-proliferation to Post-Proliferation: Explaining the U.S.-India Nuclear Deal', *Contemporary Security Policy*, 28(3), December 2007, pp. 464-493; Lisa Curtis, 'The Costs of a Failed U.S.-India Civil Nuclear Deal', web memo no. 1688, The Heritage Foundation, Washington, DC, November 2, 2007.
7. Ibid.
8. It was called the 123 agreement as it refers to Section 123 of the US Atomic Energy Act. The text of this agreement is available at: http://www.state.gov/r/pa/prs/ps/2007/aug/90050.htm.
9. George Perkovich (2010), "Global Implications of the U.S.-India Deal", *Daedalus*, 139(1), winter.
10. Ibid.
11. Carranza, Mario E. (2007), "From Non-proliferation to Post-Proliferation: Explaining the U.S.-India Nuclear Deal", *Contemporary Security Policy*, 28(3), December, pp. 464-493.
12. Carranza, Mario E. (2007), "From Non-proliferation to Post-Proliferation: Explaining the U.S.-India Nuclear Deal", *Contemporary Security Policy*, 28(3), December, pp. 464-493.
13. Paul, T.V. (2007), "The U.S.-India Nuclear Accord: Implications for the Non-Proliferation Regime", *International Journal*, 62(4), Autumn; T.V. Paul and Mahesh Shankar, "Why the U.S.-India Nuclear Accord is a Good Deal", *Survival*, 49(4), 2007, pp. 111-122.
14. Kapur, Ashok (2007), "Canada-India Nuclear Negotiations: Context and Process", in Karthika Sasikumar and Wade L.

Huntley (eds.), 'Canadian Policy on Nuclear Cooperation with India: Confronting New Dilemmas', Simons Centre for Disarmament and Non-Proliferation Research, Vancouver, p. 55.
15. Shourie, Arun (2006), "Parity, Did You Say?', *The Indian Express*, August 24.
16. Shourie, Arun (2006), "This is About Energy, Did You Say?", *The Indian Express*, August 23.
17. Karnad, Bharat (2008), "Nuclear Test is a Must', *The Asian Age*, February 22.
18. Ibid.
19. Rajaraman, R., "The India-U.S. Nuclear Deal", No. 9, pp. 67-68.
20. Rajaraman, R. (2006), "Who's Afraid of the Nuke Deal?", *The Indian Express*, February 14.
21. Basrur, Rajesh (2014), "Deterrence, Second Strike and Credibility: Revisiting India's Nuclear Doctrine", IPCS, Issue Brief, 255, July.
22. Ibid.
23. Basrur, Rajesh (2014), "Deterrence, Second Strike and Credibility: Revisiting India's Nuclear Doctrine", IPCS, Issue Brief, 255, July.
24. Ibid.
25. Ibid.
26. Basrur, Rajesh (2014), "Deterrence, Second Strike and Credibility: Revisiting India's Nuclear Doctrine", IPCS, Issue Brief, 255, July.
27. Ibid.
28. Ibid.

References

Carranza, Mario E. (2007), "From Non-proliferation to Post-Proliferation: Explaining the U.S.-India Nuclear Deal", *Contemporary Security Policy*, 28(3), December.

Chari, P.R. (2007), "Indo-US Nuclear Deal: Unending Drama in Many Acts", Institute of Peace and Conflict Studies, New Delhi.

Chari, P.R. (2014), "India's Nuclear Doctrine: Stirrings of Change", Carnegie Endowment for International Peace, Washington, D.C., June 4, available at: http://carnegieendowment.org/2014/06/04/india-s-nuclear-doctrine-stirrings-of-change/hcks.

Chellaney, Brahma (1994), "Non-proliferation: An Indian Critique of

US Export Controls", *Orbis,* 38(3), Summer.

Chellaney, Brahma (2005), "U.S. Deal is a Bad Choice for Power Generation", *The New York Times,* December 27.

Chengappa, Raj and Saurabh Shukla (2008), "Nuclear Showdown", *India Today,* March 7.

CNN News (1998), "Clinton Says India is on Wrong Side of History with Nuclear Tests", May 16.

Howard, Michael (1985), "Blackett and the Origins of Nuclear Strategy: The Blackett Memorial Lecture", *Journal of the Operational Research Society,* 36 (2): 89-95.

Joshi, Manoj (2014), "Updating India's Nuclear Posture", Observer Research Foundation, New Delhi, April 11.

Karnad, Bharat (2008), "Nuclear Test is a Must", *The Asian Age,* February 22.

Karthika, Sasikumar (2007), "India's Emergence as a 'Responsible' Nuclear Power", *International Journal,* 62(4), Autumn.

Koithara, Verghese (2012), "Managing India's Nuclear Forces", Brookings Institution Press, Washington D.C.

Menon, Raja (2014), "A Mismatch of Nuclear Doctrines", *Hindu,* January 22.

O'Donnell, Frank and Harsh V. Pant (2014), "Evolution of India's Agni-V Missile: Bureaucratic Politics and Nuclear Ambiguity", *Asian Survey,* 54(3): 584-610.

Paul, T.V. (2007), "The U.S.-India Nuclear Accord: Implications for the Non-Proliferation Regime", *International Journal,* 62(4), Autumn.

Perkovich, George (2005), "Faulty Promises: The U.S.-India Nuclear Deal", *Policy Outlook,* Carnegie Endowment for International Peace, Washington D.C., September.

Potter, William and Jayantha Dhanapala (2007), "The Perils of Non-proliferation Amnesia", *The Hindu,* September 1.

Rajaraman, R. (2006), "Who's Afraid of the Nuke Deal?", *The Indian Express,* February 14.

Rajaraman, R. (2014), "Minimum Deterrent and Large Arsenal", *The Hindu,* July 2.

Ramachandran, R. (2006), "The Complicated World of Nuclear Deals", *The Hindu,* February 9.

Ramakrishnan, Venkitesh (2010), "Empty Euphoria", *Frontline,* Chennai, December 1.

Saran, Shyam (2010), "A Premature Power", *Outlook,* Delhi,

November 2.

Saran, Shyam (2013), "Is India's Nuclear Deterrent Credible?", *Indian Review of Global Affairs*, April 25.

Sethi, Manpreet (2007), "Indo-U.S. Civilian Nuclear Cooperation: Reprocessing Issue Reconstructed", IPCS Issue Brief, No. 47, June.

Srinivasan, M.R. (2007), "A Lesson in Nuclear Reactors", *The Hindu*, September 11.

Srivastava, Anupam and Seema Gahlaut (2010), "India and the NPT: Separating Substantive Facts from Normative Fiction", *Strategic Analysis*, 34(2), March.

Subrahmanyam, K. (2007), "N-Deal Reflects New World Reality: India Must Make Use of the Opportunity", *The Tribune*, July 30.

5

Soft Power and Public Diplomacy in Foreign Policy of India

Ramanuj Hazarika

One of the oldest civilisations of the world, India has been "re-emerging" in recent times as a major player in the world, pushing behind centuries of colonial exploitation, backwardness and slumber. Many scholars believe that India's political system, its thriving democracy, military capabilities along with space and missile programme and the country's growing human resource will give it a great power status in the 21st century. Though most of these works are limited to India's hard material power, its growing soft power has a very important role to play in transforming India. The present paper would devote its attention upon the role of India's soft power in transformation of India as an emerging country of the world. The paper is basically divided into three major parts.

In the *first part,* we would investigate whether India is emerging as a major power and what are the responses from various quarters. The concept of soft power would be briefly introduced in this section and we would analyse what are the soft power resources of India and what role it has to play in the transformation of India as a major power. In the *second part,* the concept of soft power and public diplomacy would be juxtaposed and we would analyse how India has been trying to use various public diplomacy initiatives to wield its soft power resources. In the *final part,* we would investigate what are the limitations of Indian soft power and public diplomacy initiatives and how can India overcome these difficulties. The paper would also address some important questions such as—

do soft power of a particular thing such as popular culture (e.g. Bollywood) and soft power of a particular country are the same, and what is the importance of deploying public and cultural diplomacy to wield soft power resources.

Emergence of India

Despite all the problems and being "a land of contradictions" one cannot really undermine India's achievement as a nation over the last six decades. In recent years, India has been "re-emerging" as a major player in the world. Today, India is the third largest economy in terms of purchasing power parity, has the third largest military force with 1.3 million active personnel, one of the major G-20 economies, a member of BRICS and an active player in the world's politico-economic set up. The United States in its Quadrennial Defense Review (2014) has termed India's rise as an "increasingly capable actor" in the region. Not only the outside world is talking about the rise of India; Indians too are emphatic about India's growing heft in the world. According to the Global Attitude Project (2010) of Pew Research Centre, nearly nine out of ten Indians say that their country already is (38 percent) or will eventually be (49 percent) one of the most powerful nations in the world and only 8 percent just say that India will never be one of the world's leading powers.

While Shashi Tharoor (2007) calls India as the 21st century power; Mira Kamdar on the other hand (2008) believes that the world is undergoing a process of intense recalibration in which the rise of Asia is the most important factor and India holds the key to this new world. Although there have been many works regarding the rise of India, most of these works are limited to India's hard material power. However, its growing soft power has a very important role to play in the transformation of India. India, understanding the clout of soft power in the 21st century's international politics has been actively engaging in traditional, public and cultural diplomacy to wield its soft power resources.

Hitherto undefined in the field of international politics, the term "soft power" was coined by Joseph S. Nye, Jr. of Harvard University in 1990 in his book *Bound to Lead: The Changing Nature of American Power.* Though E.H. Carr described international politics in three categories: military, economic and power over opinion, which is essentially a country's soft power, he did not conceptualise the term. Nye (2004) defined it as the ability to achieve what one wants through attraction, rather than coercion. Soft power of a country emerges because of its culture, political values, foreign policies and so on. Though it will be highly parochial to call soft power as something which acts as a glove behind an iron fist and an instrument of coercion, soft power does try to "influence" public opinion, though not necessarily control it. The beauty of soft power lies in the fact that it can influence public opinion in a subtle and non-institutional way.

Despite some recent economic hiccups, India is one of the emerging powers of the 21st century. India gains a real advantageous position vis-à-vis China in competition for global attractiveness and influence due to its democratic regime type (Nye, 2004). India's economic growth, history of non-violence under the leadership of Mahatma Gandhi, independent foreign policy and Bollywood as quasi-global dream fabric are important tools that carry the formidable soft power of India. Besides India's spiritual history, ancient civilisation, yoga, ayurveda, cuisine, customs, educational institutions such as Indian Institutes of Technologies (IITs) and Indian Institutes of Managements (IIMs) and the world's most expensive cricket tournament, Indian Premier League (IPL), has contributed to an attractive image of India abroad.

Shared Heritage, Culture and Religion

Bollywood (Hindi movie industry based in Mumbai) is often considered as the epitome of Indian soft power. Indian film industry is the largest in the world, making on an average of one thousand feature films and fifteen hundred short films every year (CBFC, 2011) and the highest numbers of films in

India (nearly 20 percent) are made in Hindi. Bollywood has been able to traverse its national boundary and carry forward its aesthetic and appeal in various parts of the world including the United States, Canada, Australia, Europe, Africa, Russia, Southeast Asia, South Asia, Middle East and even in countries which do not have significant population of Indian origin. In comparison to other soft power tools, the advantage of Bollywood lies in the fact that it has the ability to transmit the values and culture of Indian society and the state across the globe in a subtle and more powerful way because of its audio-visual medium of expression.

Besides, the popularity of Bollywood actors give them great visibility and power which can be understood from the recent visit of the President of the United States Barack Obama in January 2015 when he frequently mentioned about Bollywood movies and its stars or from the Wikileaks cables of 2007 which clearly showed that US had taken a great interest in sending Bollywood stars to Afghanistan to help stabilise the troubled country and delivering anti-terrorism message. [1]

Bollywood not only provides entertainment to the people but also acts as a catalyst in the image formation of the Indian state. With India becoming a major economic player, many Bollywood movies project a modern, rising and yet traditional image of India which has been instrumental in building its distinct image. Besides, Bollywood movies also provide Indian Diaspora a link to their "root" and remind them of their "homeland".

Because of the shared heritage, culture and religion, Bollywood has greater appeal in the Arab world and India's recent economic success makes its popular culture even more appealing. Another reason for Bollywood's appeal in Islamic countries is that some of the biggest stars of Bollywood are Muslims. These success stories have profound implication in creating a secular and multicultural image of India.

Similarly, the popularity of Indian cuisine, customs and

traditions such as yoga and ayurveda and the emergence of India as a hub of software and services have not only sparked interests in the minds of millions but also helped in India's image formation. Graduates from IITs and IIMs are today dominating the technical and financial spectrums of the world and people often talk about IITs and IIMs at par with other top technical and management institutes of the world.

India has a long history of cultural and civilisational ties with Southeast Asia, Central Asia and West Asia. India's civilisational glory and richness had attracted travellers and traders for thousands of years. Buddhism spread from India to China, Japan and other distant lands leading to exchange of ideas. During the time of Ashoka, Buddhist preachers from India went to Southeast Asia to profess and propagate the values of Buddhism.

Similarly, preachers from India spread the values of Hinduism and Islam in countries such as Malaysia and Singapore. Such religious, cultural and historic ties make it easier for India to influence these countries and India's recent foreign policy strategies such as 'Look East Policy' also try to leverage by putting importance to these shared civilisational ties. Because of India's "soft" involvement in Afghanistan in the form of providing economic and logistical assistance, the country enjoys enormous goodwill in the Afghan society. According to a 2009 ABC/BBC/ARD poll, 74 percent people in Afghanistan view favourably in contrast to 91 percent of unfavourable opinions of Pakistan (Blarel, 2012: 31).

Indian Premier League (IPL) which was started in 2008 is the most popular and expensive Twenty20 cricket league in the world. Despite recent controversies like spot fixing and corruption, IPL's popularity has been growing. According to various media reports (Times of India, 2010) the brand value of IPL is $4.3 billion which is greater than the brand value of Manchester United! The development of the "Brand IPL" as an international extravaganza has also promoted "Brand India" as an advanced, developed and economic powerhouse.

Most important of all, India is a vibrant and thriving democracy, has a great civilisational history and is established on the edifice of secularism, tolerance, liberty and equality of opportunity. India can be a source of inspiration for third world countries for its successful examples of collective co-existence of different faiths, language, culture, cuisine and traditions. All these traditions and trends are directly or indirectly reflected in various popular cultures and are transmitted to audiences across the globe.

Soft Power and the Role of Indian Public Diplomacy

India has been trying to wield these soft power mechanisms through various public diplomacy initiatives. Often presumed as the most important tool of wielding soft power resources, the term public diplomacy was for the first time coined by Edmund Guillon of the Fletcher School of Law and Diplomacy in 1960s. Public diplomacy attempts to achieve foreign policy objectives by actively using soft power assets and hence, it may be seen as a contributor to the enhancement of a nation's soft power through activities such as broadcasting, communication, cultural diplomacy and exchanges. In the 21st century, the definition and scope of public diplomacy has broadened considerably and it cannot meaningfully confine to foreign publics alone. Though in the initial years, public diplomacy was used more as propaganda, in the present information and communication era, public diplomacy cannot be equated with propaganda. Information flows across boundaries and propagandas can be counterproductive. The purpose of public diplomacy is not only conveying the right message to the audience, but also to mitigate ambiguity and misunderstanding.

The pertaining question however, is that do these initiatives guarantee in wielding soft power? Though these policies may help to create an attractive image of a country and improve its prospects for obtaining desired outcomes, they may be ineffective if presented in an arrogant self-serving manner (Nye, 2004). As many experts (Nye, 2004; Pamment,

2014) believe, effective public diplomacy is a two-way process where listening and talking both are important and is embedded in mutual respect. However, we need to remember the fact that soft power resources may or may not turn into formidable soft power of a country. For example, if Bollywood conveys the ideas and principles followed by the Indian state and the receiving audiences accept it with open arms, the "soft power resources of Bollywood" will turn into "soft power of India". However, if Bollywood carries a message which the Indian state propagates, but the receiving audiences rejects it, or if Bollywood conveys ideas that are neither propagated by the Indian state nor liked by the receiving audience, the power of Bollywood may result turn into a boomerang. Hence, the soft power of Bollywood is one thing and using soft power of Bollywood as soft power of India is another.

India has been trying to use public diplomacy and soft power to secure its foreign policy objectives since the time of its Independence, although the methods hugely vary in different time periods. After Independence, though India lacked formidable hard power resources, it had considerable amount of soft power because of its ancient tradition, freedom struggle, history of non-violence and so on. Besides, India took a leadership role in initiating the non-aligned movement, invested heavily in high-level dialogues, cultural exchanges and conferences along with trying to influence different people and governments through diplomacy and moral suasion (Hall, 2012).

As a result of exponential economic rise, increasing soft power resources and de-facto recognition of nuclear power status by the United States and other powers after the Indo-US nuclear deal of 2005, the perception of India is boosted manifold in the international community and in such a scenario, wielding soft power through public diplomacy has become more crucial for India. As Ian Hall (2012) observes, the new public diplomacy of India while building upon this tradition, departs from the past in broadly three ways. First, Indian public diplomacy seeks new audiences at home, among Diaspora and in the developing world.

Second, Indian foreign policy making process and public diplomacy initiative are now more open and democratic than before. Third, there is an increasing effort to utilise new media rather than traditional ones. Besides, Nehru's India which tried to use its soft power without any formidable hard power, the India of the present era speaks softly and also carries a big stick in the form of hard power.

India carries forward its public diplomacy initiatives through various ministries and organisations including Ministry of External Affairs, Ministry of Overseas Indian Affairs and Ministry of Information and Broadcasting among many others.

Public Diplomacy Division of Ministry of External Affairs

India has invested significant resources in public diplomacy over the last decade. In contrast to previous efforts, India's new public diplomacy seeks to utilise new media rather than traditional methods to reach its various target audiences. [2] The Public Diplomacy Division (PDD) within Ministry of External Affairs (MEA) aims to "educate and influence global and domestic opinion on key policy issues and project a better image of the country commensurate with its rising international standing". It attempts to reach out to overseas Indians, build connections with foreign business interests, initiate development cooperation programmes and, use major events to showcase "nation-brand" India.

PDD's function ranges from production of print and audio-visual materials depicting diverse tradition and culture to organising a wide range of outreach activities aimed at creating a greater understanding of India and its foreign policy, both within and outside India. To achieve these objectives, PDD also collaborates with major national and international universities, think tanks, research organisations, and chambers of commerce in organising seminars and conferences relevant to India's national interests (Suri, 2011).

Almost all the documentaries that were produced by MEA since 1981 have been uploaded on its YouTube channel (MEA,

2012-2013). Currently, it is undertaking campaigns such as "India Global", "India Is...", "India Africa-A Shared Future" and "India File". PDD also helps diplomatic missions in organising Indian film festivals with the aim to utilise film's soft power potential. To mark 60 years of India's independence, PDD also issued three videos on Bollywood, namely *Made in Bollywood, Bollywood: 60 Years of Romance* and *Hindi in Bollywood,* although the phrase "soft power" was not used by MEA (Thussu, 2013).

Besides, PDD also commissions documentary films on a wide range of issues to portray various facets of India. [3] PDD publishes coffee table books like *India for a Billion Reasons* and *India-Spirit of Enterprise* in English, Russian, French, Arabic, Spanish and Portuguese. *India Perspective* magazine which is published in 17 languages and distributed in over 150 countries in the world is an attempt to promote India's image as a multicultural and tolerant democracy.

Activities of Indian Council of Cultural Relations (ICCR)

India's image cultivation and promotion is also done by the ICCR through the instrument of cultural diplomacy. The important activities of ICCR includes administration of scholarship schemes for overseas students on behalf of Government of India and other agencies, exhibitions, participation in major cultural festivals abroad, exchange of groups of performing artists, establishing and operating Chairs for Indian studies in universities abroad, presentation of books, audio visual material, art objects and musical instruments to institutions abroad, publication of journals, operation of Indian Cultural Centres overseas and regional offices within India, to synergize with other cultural institutions in foreign countries and to undertake projects on behalf of MEA. It publishes six journals in five different languages, namely, *India Horizons* and *Africa Quarterly* (English, quarterly); *Gaganachal* (Hindi, bimonthly), *Papeles de la India* (Spanish, half-yearly); *Rencontre Avec L' Inde* (French, half-yearly) and *Thaqafat-ul-Hind* (Arabic, quarterly).

Activities of the Ministry of Information and Broadcasting

The Ministry of Information and Broadcasting (MIB) also lends support to the public diplomacy initiative through strategic use of media. It is the apex body for formulation and administration of rules and regulations relating to information, broadcasting, press and films in India and its mandates include news service through All India Radio (AIR) and Doordarshan (DD), development of broadcasting and television, import and export of films, development and promotion of film industry, organisation of film festivals and cultural exchanges, handling of press relations regards the policies of government and getting feedback and dissemination of information about India within and outside the country through various publications of national importance.

The Films Division, the premier central film producing organisation of the Government of India is under MIB and is empowered to produce documentaries, short fiction films and other films on behalf of various ministries for nation-branding efforts. Since its inception in 1975, National Film Development Corporation (NFDC) has been the apex agency in film financing, production and distribution in India. It is also marketing Indian feature films in overseas market through platforms like International Film festivals in Cannes and Berlin. NFDC and its forerunner Film Finance Corporation (FFC) have till now produced more than 300 films in various Indian languages some of which (*Ek Doctor Ki Maut, Anhe Ghore Da Daan, Jaane Bhi Do Yaro, Train to Pakistan*) are widely regarded as classics of all time. It was also one of the producers of the movie *Gandhi* (1982) which won eight Academy Awards in 1983. NFDC, in 2013 under a new initiative, started its label "Cinemas of India" to promote and distribute parallel cinema produced by it since 1960s. Recognising the growing digitalisation of data and role of social media, many of these movies are made freely available online.

The Song and Drama Division of the Ministry, on the

other hand, seeks to create awareness and emotional receptivity among the general public regarding social, economic and democratic ideals that are conducive to the progress of the nation. The Directorate of Films Festival (DFF) has the responsibility of promoting aesthetically and technically excellent movies both within and outside the country through International Film Festivals of India (IFFI), organisation of film festivals and film weeks and through National Film Awards.

Indian government is involved in the nation-branding campaigns such as "Incredible India" or "Brand India" to build positive perception of India internationally. Other notable campaigns are "Pravasi Bharatiya Divas" and "Know India" programme conducted by Ministry of Overseas Indian Affairs (MOIA), designed to provide the Indian Diaspora with a link to their "roots". The PDD has also tied up with the "INDIA-future of change" (IFC) initiativc that seeks to emphasise India's position as a catalyst of change. Indian Council of World affairs (ICWA) plays an another important role in producing and disseminating research on foreign affairs, holding seminars and publishing one major journal, *India Quarterly.*

One of the largest recipients of foreign aid, India with its economic rise has also emerged as a major donor country of the world. In the new millennium, India's limited development cooperation programme is supplemented by targeted technical assistance, where much of this money goes to Africa and Afghanistan. [4]

Limitations of Soft Power and Public Diplomacy Initiatives

While there are some bright sides of India's soft power, there are also some inherent limitations of it. Soft power is difficult to wield, compared to hard power for the reason that many of the crucial resources are outside the control of government and their effects heavily depend on acceptance by receiving audiences (Nye, 2004). For example, production of feature films is mostly in the hands of the private sector. There is hardly any government control or regulation during production, except in case of films produced by government agencies such as Doordarshan or NFDC where they approve the story in advance (CBFC, 2011). In 2011, CBFC certified 1,255 Indian films, while only 13 Indian feature films and 2 foreign feature films were initially refused certificate. Even subsequently, some of the feature films were passed by Film Certification Appellate Tribunal (FCAT) or by CBFC in revised or re-revised versions (CBFC, 2011).

As M.K. Raghavendra (2012) argues, although a new kind of soft power exercised by brand Bollywood is clearly visible, Bollywood exercises it largely on its own behalf unlike the popular Hindi films which once exercised soft power on behalf of India. In a survey conducted by David J. Schaefer (2013), it was found that the highest grossing Hindi films produced after 1991 exhibit significantly higher exogenous content including modern and urban social institutions, practices and Western cultural content than those produced beforehand. As Schaefer (2013) has argued, despite the fact that audiences of Bollywood movies are increasing outside India, if this rise is eventually coupled with a significant decrease in the indigenous content, it may actually serve the needs of multinational corporations rather than the Indian government.

If Bollywood has soft power, Indian state doesn't have monopoly over it. Not only the Indian government tries to take advantage of the growing popularity of Bollywood, but a number of international organisations and countries have sought to use the global influence of Bollywood to project a positive image about them. Amitabh Bachchan, Sharmila Tagore, Priyanka Chopra, Aamir Khan, Raveena Tandon and Nandana Sen are supporting UNICEF's work for women and children in India. As Shashi Tharoor has argued, if Bollywood contributes to the soft power of India then it also contributes to the soft power of those who piggyback on a globalised Bollywood.

The popularity and attractiveness of India's popular culture such as Bollywood should not be confused with its ability to set political agenda for the nation. The popularity of Indian films in Pakistan did not reduce hostilities across the border nor prevented the terrorist attacks. This however, coincides with the fact that the Indian government has put little importance to deploy cultural diplomacy in Pakistan. Despite having cultural similarity and close geographical proximity, surprisingly ICCR has no presence in Pakistan.

Inability of Bollywood to accommodate different cultures of India and people also decreases its soft power potential. Most Bollywood movies portray a universal image of "Indian culture", basically rooted in North India and "construct" a stereotypical identity of North-East and South India. The entire North-Eastern India is hardly ever represented in Bollywood movies and if the region occasionally appears, rather than showing its culture and traditions as part of Indian culture it portrays the region mainly as a disturbed area. Besides, many movies are highly insensitive towards the "different" look and habits of the people of the region. [5]

Though some films like *Chak De India* (2007) tries to fit the people of North-East in the narratives of Indianness, in most of the films the issue is still unaddressed. When Bollywood indirectly promotes such kind of indifferent and insensitive attitude towards tradition and culture of some part of India, increasing chances are there that such attitude would also be reflected in the behaviour of people. If soft power is "not what one shows, rather what one actually is", then the division of Indian society and the resulted conflict can only harm India's soft power potential. The idea of India which is rooted in diversity can best be portrayed if Bollywood represents different region's culture as an integral part of the composite Indian culture.

If Bollywood is sensitive towards North-East, why don't filmmakers expand their horizons and look for actors from the region, rather than those from the South and North India, or do the people of this region not fit in the cultural imagination of India?

Probably this is the reason why the Ladakhi character of Phonstok Wangdu in *3 Idiots* (2009) was played by Amir Khan, Tibetan character of Tashi Dorjee Lhatoo by Imran Khan in *Delhi Belly* (2011) or the biopic on Mary Kom (2014) by Priyanka Chopra. Reacting to a question on why there have been fewer faces from North-East in Bollywood, Danny Denzongpa once replied to a *Times of India* correspondent (2013), "It is an industry. They don't cast faces from the North-east because it will not sell. I am probably here because I have some Aryan features".

Indian public diplomacy is still in a nascent stage and the country had established a separate Public Diplomacy Division only in 2006. Till February 2015, the ICCR had only 35 cultural centres and 2 sub-centres outside India and 20 regional centres within the country. This is despite the fact that ICCR was established as far back as 1950. ICCR does not have a cultural centre even in important countries like the United States, Canada, France and Pakistan. In contrast, China had established Confucius Institutes only in 2004 to promote Chinese language and culture, and despite this right now it has more than 500 Confucius Institutes all around the globe and by 2020 it plans to establish 1,000 Confucius Institutes. India's state media presence is still underdeveloped compared to countries such as US and China. Besides, India's state media presence is still underdeveloped compared to countries such as US and China.

Indian Foreign Service's (IFS) numerical strength is abysmally small. India has only 600 frontline Foreign Service officers in 162 diplomatic missions compared to 5,000 in China and 10,000 in the US. IFS lacks the numerical strength to project India's influence in a manner befitting as an emerging power and Naresh Chandra Task Force Report of 2012 pointed out that the IFS doesn't have enough diplomats to "anticipate, analyze and act on contemporary challenges". If India desires to be a global power, it has to address these issues.

Though there are both positive and negative stories about any country, as argued by the former head of PDD Navdeep Suri (2011), the negative stories about India are most highlighted both in traditional and new age media and hence, there is a pressing need to start speaking about all the positive work that India has been doing through its development partnerships in Africa, Southeast Asia, Latin America and in India's own neighbourhood. Suri holds that creating a space for conversation and narratives about real work can never be propaganda. Public diplomacy by doing so would try to amplify actual stories in a way that they provide countervailing narrative to the dominant theme of negativism.

One of the greatest challenges towards India's soft power is its internal problems. Issues that are currently prevailing in India such as poverty, casteism, terrorism, militancy, religious fundamentalism, corruption, gender-based violence and alleged human rights abuse by security forces would not allow India to leverage its soft power. Unless and until the country is able to solve its domestic issues, no matter what image India's soft power resources carries to the outside world, it would remain ineffective.

Conclusion

This paper attempted to understand the role of soft power in India's rise. However, overemphasis on the role of soft power is in no way the objective. We are well aware about a range of limitations of soft power. As Joseph Nye himself has claimed, soft power or hard power alone cannot fulfil a nation's aspirations and to have successful foreign policy, there has to be perfect use of both hard power and soft power, what is now known as "smart power". The recent example of US involvement in Iraq proves beyond doubt that states cannot overemphasise on hard power. Rather than building a peaceful and stable democracy, the US involvement in Iraq has given birth to a monster called ISIS.

Another problem with soft power is the fact that a soft power measure which we regard as less relevant today may reveal its relevance and produce unanticipated positive outcomes in the long-term. However, we should remember that soft power acts most effectively when there is a certain degree of interaction and interchange of values between different actors. It acts most effectively only when the receiver accepts it gracefully.

If India wants to be an attraction for others, it not only has to provide basic facilities to all its citizens, but also has to follow the precious pluralism and respect, rooted in civilisational history of the country. If India doesn't solve these problems and accommodate and give equal "respect" (rather than to tolerate) to each and every community, no amount of soft power can help it to become a world leader. As Sunil Khilnani (2004) has argued, the greatest asset of India is the "accumulated political legitimacy" which, rather than any hypothetical or real accumulation of power, lies at the core of soft power for any state. To achieve a positive image, India has to utilise its cultural attraction, publish its achievements and contributions, send the right messages, reach out to its Diaspora and, most importantly, build a greater coherence between domestic and foreign policy.

Endnotes

1. WikiLeaks cable (March 28, 2007, Canonical Id: 07NEWDELHI1485_a) stated that the US had taken a great interest in sending Bollywood stars to Afghanistan to help stabilise the troubled country. In another cable (October 25, 2007, Canonical Id: 07LONDON4045_a) it is said that US officials have met with a cross section of South Asian community to discuss the potential of working with Bollywood on delivering anti-terrorism message. In the same cable it is also mentioned that Bollywood actors and executives had agreed with the United States Government to promote anti-extremist messages through third party actors and were excited about the idea of possible partnering of Hollywood as well.
2. For innovative use of technology in the sphere of digital

diplomacy under the category of "public participative initiative", PDD received the Webratna Awards in 2012 as "Platinum Icon" from the Ministry of Information and Broadcasting.

3. During 2012-2013, a number of documentaries were made. Some of them are "Indian Diaspora" (Canada), "Sound Check, A New Beginning India-US Relationships", "Tana-Bana-the Wrap and Weft of India", "Chinese Investment in India", "Harmony Fest", "Spirit of Freedom in India" and "India-ASEAN Relations" (MEA, 2012-2013).
4. Since 2003, nearly $10 billion in credit has been made available to Africa. Afghanistan on the other hand, receives billions of dollars from India. India has also assisted Afghanistan to develop its infrastructure and transport sector.
5. For example, in *Band Baaja Baaraat* (2010) when the male protagonist of the film, Bittoo Sharma (Ranveer Singh) goes to receive some guests of a wedding to the airport, he taunts them in front of the female protagonist Shruti Kakkar (Anushka Sharma) as "chinkies", a racial slur which is generally used against the people of North-East.

References

Blarel, Nicolas (2012), "India's Soft Power: From Potential to Reality?" in 'India: The Next Superpower?', IDEAS Special Report, London: London School of Economics, available at: http://www.clingendael.nl/sites/default/files/20080100_cdsp_paper_berger.pdf.

Central Board of Film Certification, Ministry of Information and Broadcasting, Government of India (2011), "Annual Report", available at: http://cbfcindia.gov.in/CbfcWeb/fckeditor/editor/images/Uploadedfiles/file/Publications/ANNUAL_2011.pdf.

Department of Defense, United States of America (2014), "Quadrennial Defense Review", available at: http://www.defense.gov/pubs/2014_Quadrennial_Defense_Review.pdf.

Hall, Ian (2012), "India's New Public Diplomacy: Soft Power and the Limits of Government Action", *Asian Survey*, 52(6): 1089-1110.

Kamdar, Mira (2008), "Planet India: How the Fastest-Growing Democracy is Transforming America and the World", Scribner,

New York.

Khilnani, Sunil (2004), "The Idea of India", Penguin Books, New Delhi.

Ministry of External Affairs, Government of India (2012-2013), "Annual Report", available at: http://www.mea.gov.in/Uploads/PublicationDocs/21385_Annual_Report_2012 2013_English.pdf.

Ministry of Information and Broadcasting, Government of India (2013-2014), "Outcome Budget", available at: http://www.performance.gov.in/sites/default/files/departments/info-broad/Outcome%20Budget%202013-14.pdf.

Nye, Joseph S. Jr. (2004), "Soft Power: The Means to Success in World Politics", Public Affairs, New York.

—-(2008), "Public Diplomacy and Soft Power", *Annals of the American Academy of Political and Social Science*, 61(6): 94-109.

Pamment, James (2013), "New Public Diplomacy in the 21st Century: A Comparative Study of Policy and Practice", Routledge, Oxon.

Pew Research Center (2010), "Indians See Threat from Pakistan, Extremist Groups", *Global Attitude Project,* available at: http://www.pewglobal.org/files/2010/10/Pew-Global-Attitudes-India-Report-FINAL-October-20-2010.pdf.

Raghavendra, M.K. (2012), "Mainstream Hindi Cinema and Brand Bollywood: The transformation of a Cultural Artefact", in Anjali Gera Roy (eds.), 'The Magic of Bollywood: At Home and Abroad', Sage Publications, New Delhi.

Schaefer, David J. and Kavita Karan (2013), "Bollywood and Globalisation: The Global Power of Popular Hindi Cinema", Routledge, London and New York.

Suri, Navdeep (2011), "Public Diplomacy in India's Foreign Policy", *Strategic Analysis,* 35(2): 297-303.

Tharoor, Shashi (2007), "The Elephant, the Tiger, and the Cellphone: Reflections on India in the 21st Century", Penguin Books, New Delhi.

—-(2012), "PAX INDICA India and the World in the 21st Century", Allen Lane, New Delhi.

Times of India (2010), "IPL Brand Value Doubles to $4.13 billion: Study", available at: http://timesofindia.indiatimes.com/ipl/news/IPL-brand-value-doubles-to-4-13-billion-Study/articleshow/5713042.cms.

Thussu, Daya Kishan (2006), "Contra-Flow in Global Media: An Asian Perspective", paper presented at the AMIC Annual Conference on Media in Asia: Aspirations, Choices and Realities, Penang, Malaysia, available at: http://www.amic.org.sg/Resources/Research_Materials/Broadcasting/Contra%20Flow%20in%20Global%20Media%20An%20Asian%20Perspective.pdf.

—–(2013), "Communicating India's Soft Power: From Buddha to Bollywood", Palgrave Macmillan, New York.

WikiLeaks (2007), "Opportunities for Indian Soft power in Afghanistan", Canonical Id: 07NEWDELHI1485_a. 28 March 12: 06 Wednesday, available at: https://wikileaks.org/plusd/cables/07NEWDELHI1485_a.html.

—–(2007), "Eur Senior Advisor Pandith and S/P Advisor Cohen's Visit to the UK", Canonical Id: 07LONDON4045_a. 25th October,16: 38 Thursday, available at: https://wikileaks.org/plusd/cables/07LONDON4045_a.html.

6

India's Foreign Policy and Regional Multilateralism in South Asia

Suresh K.

The increasing proliferation of regional economic cooperation is a major development in the international political economy after the Second World War. Both the North and the South have engaged in the process of creating regional trading agreements and organizations for economic and social development. It helps to bring hostile countries together on a common platform, the classical example being the States in European Union and Southeast Asia, where economic dimensions have brought long standing foes in the same fora. As far as third world states, especially South Asia, are concerned, despite the existence of a favourable regional and international environment, it failed to create an effective regional framework. The paper therefore, attempts to address two questions:

1. Whether economic compulsions will drive South Asian countries towards greater cooperation and development and if so what role India could play in the changed economic milieu?
2. To what extent South Asian countries are able to achieve economic interdependence keeping aside their long history of mutual hostility and mistrust.

Multilateralism has been increasingly recognised as the modus operandi in international political arena since the Second World War. The aim was to strengthen the smaller and weaker states in their bilateral relations with the industrially developed economies. Multilateral institutions like UNO, ICJ,

World Bank, IMF, WTO, etc. were born out of the concept of multilateralism. But in this new world order, United States of America, being the centre of gravity of the global economy—both politically and economically—began to define the rules of multilateral game. The global South, comprising primarily of developing and underdeveloped states, can do nothing but only to accept the rules formulated by the North.

However, situation has changed dramatically in recent years with the emergence of new emerging economies which pose a serious challenge to existing economic order structured by the United States. Their economic and political influence enabled them to take an independent stand on various issues. They wanted more participation in reshaping the world economic order in accordance with their national interest. The best pragmatist approach therefore is to apply the universal, uniform and equal framework of multilateralism to a regional scale.

The formation of regional groupings has both national and international consequences. Many of regionalism drivers and barriers are shaped by factors such as fragmentation and size constraints, the role of international political coordination and governance, matters related to national economic and political interests, as well as power and the distribution of wealth and resources in both regions and countries (Soderbaum and Granit, 2014). The complexity of today's regionalism emphasises the need for adopting a broad and interdisciplinary approach for understanding regionalism.

Economic studies generally place little emphasis on the political conditions that shape regionalism. The formation of regional organisations, therefore, has to be considered from a political economy perspective. There is an increasing belief that governments are acting to maximise social welfare and as such they are immune from domestic pressures. The political economy approach takes into account the interaction between economic policies, domestic politics and strategic interaction between governments. Political factors have an undesirable influence upon various trading policies. The commercial policy of a country is determined on the basis of the strength of pressure groups, rather than on the aggregate welfare considerations (Kreinin ME and Plummer, 1993).

Political Economy of Regional Multilateralism

The formation of regional economic groupings has become a significant change in the world economy in the post-Cold war period. It has been widely accepted among the developed and developing countries that mutual cooperation and common action are essential for the accomplishment of development goals. Various recent studies indicate that whether states choose to enter regional trade and arrangement and the economic effects of these arrangements depend on the preference of national policy makers and interest groups, as well as the nature and strength of domestic institutions (Mansfield and Milner, 1999).

Though most economists and policy analysts argue in favour of unilateral trade liberalisations, policy makers find it difficult to transform this view to reality due to political constraints (Ali and Talukder, 2010). Conflicts among various trading groups within a country or a region play an important role in shaping trade policy. Capital owners and labourers in importing competing industries are usually effective in lobbying to retain or increase protection, as their gains from protection are reasonably transparent.

On the other hand, export-oriented producers and consumers favour less protection. There are many benefits accruing from regional multilateralism like regional interdependence, speeding up economic growth, ameliorating poverty, raising employment levels etc. It helps to reduce growth gaps between developing countries through regional trade integration, close financial linkage, supply chains as well as speed up growth of slow economies (Pant et al., 2014). In order to achieve equitable growth, nations acquire extended markets, together with advancement in infrastructure, energy and connectivity and integration into international system. These solutions are particularly relevant for developing countries where they find it difficult to find large scale infrastructural projects, making regional approach more conducive.

The present international economic situation, characterised by stagnant growth, recessionary conditions and protectionist tendencies in the developed countries has seriously underpinned the economic growth in developing Countries (Chawla, 1991). The worsening terms of trade, acute balance of payment crisis and debt burden on developing countries have further crippled the potential economic growth of these countries. Therefore, current world conditions underscore the need for a greater economic co-operation among the developing countries.

Political Economy of South Asia

South Asia occupies a unique position in international system since the beginning of the post-War period and it retains its importance even in the post-Cold war period. South Asia comprises seven states: Bangladesh, Bhutan, India, Maldives, Nepal, Pakistan, and Sri Lanka. Afghanistan became a member of the region in 2005. The region is spread over an area of half a million square kilometres, inhabited by 22 percent of world's population i.e., 1.67 billion people. Among this population more than 1 billion people live in India. The estimated GDP generated by all the South Asian nations constitute about US$ 2.370 Trillion (World Bank, 2013). All the nations in the region have an economy that is basically agricultural. Over 75-80 percent of the people depended on land for their living (Gupta, 1996). Currently all the countries in the region are engaged in developing industries based on indigenous raw materials. The region has been at the centre stage of global attention due to its complex security issues, internal conflicts, intrusion of global power, untapped economic resources, strategic importance of its location and the birth of two nuclear powers having positioned against each other. South Asia, as a whole, is under extreme poverty, mega urbanisation, growing disparity between the rich and the poor and issues related to infrastructure, energy and environment (Delinic, 2011).

The South Asian states have a long and closely shared history. They are having shared commonalities in terms of culture, ethnicity, and religion. There are often cross-border similarities in tradition, language, and customs. South Asia is an aboard for more than twenty major world languages and various regional dialects. Adherents of every major world religion are to be found in the subcontinent. Hinduism, Buddhism, Islam, Christians, Jains, Zoroastrians, Sikhs etc. have played a vital role in the culture and politics of the region.

The interaction of religions in the area gives rise to a feeling of solidarity among various religions which transcends national boundaries. Thus, the Muslims in Pakistan have sympathy with the Muslims in India. Similarly, the common religion in Burma and Sri Lanka has led to the manifestation of religious bounds. The Hindu Tamils in Sri Lanka find their support in South India. However, religious bonds have failed to alleviate political stresses. In fact, religious differences have combined with economic factors to create political disputes in the region (Hasan, 1964). Thus Hindu-Muslim tensions in India and Hindu-Buddhist conflict in Sri Lanka have contributed to strained relations between Pakistan and India, and Sri Lanka and India respectively.

Almost the entire region was under British colonialism for a substantial portion of their history. In the early 20th century, the political boundaries of South Asia were redrawn into a number of independent states. Even after political independence, most of the states failed to ensure democratic freedom for its vast majority of people. Democracy, authoritarianism, military-cum-fundamentalist rule, monarchy etc. were periodically experimented. South Asia is therefore, a mixed bag of governmental forms which falls under four categories: India and Sri Lanka as democratic; Bangladesh and Pakistan as clouds and sunshine states, meaning, alternatively democratic and military dictatorship; Bhutan and Nepal as monarchical and Maldives as single party authoritarianism (Ghosh, 2006).

In some countries, democratic freedom is altogether unknown; but even in countries where civil liberties are guaranteed by constitution, large patches of autocratic, arbitrary and feudalistic practices vitiate the area of governance (Gupta, 2000). Even after its long journey of democracy, India still is under the vestiges of colonialism. Its police and military are still considered as a coercive apparatus used to terrorise people and thereby undermining democratic consensus building. Therefore, despite successful institutionalization, democracy has failed to secure substantial changes in people's life. In Sri Lanka, due to the ethnic strife between majority Sinhalese and minority Tamilians, the state has to divert its resources for military manoeuvre and thereby completely neglected the genuine needs of its citizens. Nepal and Bangladesh had also experienced long periods of despotic, dynastic, or military rule until widespread popular discontent culminated in the growth of democratic process. But experience in South Asia demonstrated that institution of representative government does not necessarily create a climate for responsible government (Gupta, Ibid).

In spite of these common factors, no strong desire exists among the nations to sacrifice their sovereignty and come together to form a large unit. It has been advocated by a number of people that a sense of regional unity should be promoted in South Asia with the ultimate aim of integrating the various countries into a larger union. It is argued that common historical bonds will serve as a unifying factor. If conditions in South Asia are viewed analytically, it is crystal clear that 'the critical ingredient as seen most saliently in Europe, is political solidarity, which, unfortunately, is absent in South Asia (Maskay, 2003). The difference between the various states is too great to permit a close union.

South Asia is also noted for its multiple inter-state and intra-state regional disputes based on geographical boundaries or narrow considerations of religion, caste, language or ethnicity (Kher, 2012). Among the states of South Asia, India has bilateral disputes with most of the states due to its geographical and economic position. These unending conflicts have resulted in trust deficit between members of the region and thus act as greatest barrier to effective regional co-operation. The conspicuous example is the bilateral relationship between India and Pakistan. The differences in the models of nation-building and the political and administrative system have resulted in animosity and trust deficit between them. As a result, two wars were fought in 1965 and 1971 over the issue of Kashmir and independence of Bangladesh respectively. They are also engaged in massive arms race and propaganda against each other.

India's relationship with Bangladesh and Sri Lanka are beset by gaps in trust. Once the close friend of India, Bangladesh has changed over years. Dispute between the two countries is over the question of illegal inflow of migrants, demarcation of boundaries, and sharing of the Ganges water. The differences between Sri Lanka and India is on the nationality of Tamilians, where Sri Lanka accused India, especially the state Government of Tamil Nadu for supplying arms and providing training to the Tamil terrorists in its southern areas (Haider, 2001). The dispute between India and Nepal is on the issue of open border and the Indo-Nepal Treaty of Peace and Friendship of July 1950. Bhutan and Maldives, being very small in economic and political power, play only a minimal role in South Asian economy and polity. These complex inter-state disputes between the members of the region are a major stumbling block towards effective multilateralism in South Asia.

Regarding human development index, all SAARC countries have a low ranking on the Human Development Index (Table 6.1).

South Asia is one of the most dynamic regions in the world in terms of its geo-strategic position and huge untapped economic potential. But it remains as the least economically integrated region. The intra-regional trade accounts for only 4 percent as compared to other regional trading blocs like EU, NAFTA, and ASEAN etc. (Table 6.2). Consequently, interdependence of these economies is quiet limited.

Table 6.1: SAARC Countries' Human Development Index

SI. No	World Index	Country	HDI
1.	73	Sri Lanka	0.75
2.	103	Maldives	0.698
3.	135	India	0.586
4.	136	Bhutan	0.584
5.	142	Bangladesh	0.588
6.	145	Nepal	0.540
7.	146	Pakistan	0.537
8.	169	Afghanistan	0.468

Source: Human Development Report, 2014.

Table 6.2: Intra-regional Trade of Major Trading Blocks

Regional Organisations	Intra-regional Trade (percent)
European Union	67
North American Free Trade Area	62
Association of Southeast Asian Nations	26
Common Market For Eastern and Southern Africa	22
Latin America and Caribbean	22
Gulf Co-operation Council	8
South Asia	4

Source: World Bank, *South Asia: Growth and Regional Integration*, Washington D.C., 2007.

Regarding the intra-regional trade between various SAARC countries, as of September 20, 2013, the total value of exports by member states under SAFTA had reached about US$ 3 billion (SAARC Secretariat, 2013). Even though South

Asia's trade with both its sub-regional and external partners has increased significantly since 1990s, trade growth with external partners has been much faster. As indicated in Table 6.3, intra sub-regional trade share increased from US$ 1.8 billion in 1990 to US$ 40.6 billion in 2011, whereas South Asian trade with the outside world increased from US$ 66.2 billion in 1990 to US$ 961.1 billion $ in 2011. This shows that all South Asian economies depended heavily on market outside the region as their export destination (Table 6.3).

Four reasons can be attributed to this limited intra-regional trade; first, most of the South Asian countries, being primary producers, tend to export similar items and thus compete with each other; second, the South Asian countries, with the exception of Sri Lanka, have a high rate of tariff and non-tariff barriers, which is the most important constraining factor for the expansion of intra-regional trade; third, lack of adequate transport and information links among the South Asian countries poses serious problem for the expansion of intra-regional trade.

Table 6.3: South Asia's Total Trade with the Sub-region and the World

South Asia				World	
Year	Total trade (US$ billion)	Percent of South Asia's total trade with world	Total trade growth	Total trade (US$ billion)	Total trade growth
1990	1.8	2.7	N.A.	66.2	N.A.
1995	4.4	4.2	43.3	104.4	26.9
2000	6.2	4.3	21.7	142.6	10.6
2005	17.3	5.3	30.6	324.1	32.5
2010	33.2	4.6	45.9	719.9	33.8
2011	40.5	4.3	22.1	951.1	32.1

Source: Asia Regional Integration Center (ARIC), *Integration Indicators Database*, available at:
http://aric.adb.org/indicator.php, accessed December 20, 2014.

Finally political differences and the lack of willingness to create trade complementarities among the leaders of South Asian countries contribute to the current low level of intra-regional trade (Das, 1996). Above all, the political issues between India and Pakistan, is the single formidable challenge in intra-regional trade in South Asia. Therefore, political conflicts as well as differences in economic perceptions have been strong impediments to intra-regional trade in South Asia (Din and Nasir, 2005).

Regional Multilateralism in South Asia

Inspired by the success of regional integration in other parts of the world and the growing protectionist tendencies in the international markets, there is an imperative need for regional economic co-operation in South Asia. At present, there are four regional initiatives in South Asia and its neighbouring regions—South Asian Association for Regional Cooperation, Bay of Bengal Initiative for Multi Sectoral Economic Cooperation, Indian Ocean Rim Association for Regional Cooperation, and the Mekong Ganga Cooperation Initiative (Michael, 2013). It was argued that increasing regional economic co-operation would help to reduce the economic dependence of South Asian countries on the developed world. Given the possibility that trade with the rest of the world does not offer very happy prospects in the future, South Asian countries are now moving towards intra-regional co-operation for self-reliant growth and development.

As far as South Asia is concerned, it is considered feasible since intra-regional, historical, cultural, geographical and developmental commonalities are much stronger than differences in political and economic structures and institutions. It was upon this premise that, though being late, SAARC was formed in 1985. SAARC is considered as a manifestation of the determination of the people of South Asia to work together towards finding solutions to their common problems in a spirit of friendship, trust, and understanding and to create an order based on mutual respect, equity and shared benefits. The primary objective of the Association is the acceleration of the process of economic and social development of member states through collective action in agreed areas of co-operation.

After a decade of establishment of SAARC, a regional economic co-operation agreement called SAPTA came into existence in 1995. This agreement is considered as a stepping stone towards further economic co-operation among SAARC countries. SAPTA was expected to provide its member's preferential treatment by way of reducing way of import tariff on eligible items (Pant et al., 2014). In 2006, another bold initiative was at the regional level by the adoption of a new agreement called SAFTA, which officially came into existence in 2006. It aims to reduce tariff to 0 to 5 percent over a ten year period. It provides member countries like India, Pakistan and Sri Lanka to set their customs tariff under 5 percent by 2013, whereas it allowed the LDCs of the region namely Afghanistan, Bangladesh, Bhutan, Maldives and Nepal longer time frame to reduce or eliminate tariff by 2016.

The institutional achievements have done little in materializing effective regionalism due the intense bilateral disputes and the increasing economic asymmetry. The belated start and slow growth of regional cooperation in South Asia is the direct consequence of the lack of political commitment as a result of the bilateral disputes (Bhargava et al., 1995). Relationship between India and Pakistan manifest the lack of political commitment and trust. The two states have been locked in perpetual conflict—either overt or covert—since they gained Independence in 1947, constituting the single largest constraint to regional economic integration (Moeed, 2007). If political disputes are amicably settled the region it can ensure economic development through interdependence. The economic asymmetry has also made the political economy of the region unfavourable to regional cooperation (Hossain and Duncan, 1998).

India's economic domination and regional aspirations have created much psyche and apprehension in her neighbours which proved to be a major obstacle to effective multilateralism. Therefore, it is up to India to create an effective environment of mutual cooperation by instilling confidence in her neighbours by recognizing the unevenness in the region. Improved political understanding will result in minimizing the trust deficit and thus the enormous amount spent on military expenditure can be effectively used for the socio-economic development of the millions of people in the region. Even though, SAFTA has generated many expectations, there were concerns about its success with the emergence of more liberal free trade agreements as well as preferential access that could be granted through alternative trading agreements among SAARC countries (Pant et al., 2014).

India's South Asian Policy: Need for Reforms

India occupies a unique position among the South Asian countries due to its territorial size, large population, rapid pace of economic growth and its foreign policy ideas. Pakistan, Bangladesh, Sri Lanka, Maldives are situated at the periphery of the subcontinent in which India is the central power. Since India is the only country having physical proximity with all other South Asian nations, it acts as a geographical connectivity between the members of the region. India accounts for 73.4 percent of the territory, 76.5 percent of the population and 97.2 percent of the GNP (Bratersky and Lunyov, 1990). In the military field also, she has some asymmetrical advantages compared to other states in South Asia. India's geo-strategic position and military dominance have a substantial role in determining the regional situation. With its ability to establish alliances, both military and economic, and with its foreign policy strategy, she has begun to play as a real regional power.

Therefore, without the effective support and co-operation, there has been no possibility of inter-state trade and commerce, people-to-people contact, energy security or any other regional initiatives. But it should not be undermined that India's prominence has been one of the many hurdles standing in the way of South Asia's integration.

The main goal of India's foreign policy, since Independence, has been the establishment of peace, security and development within its borders. From this point of view, it has always given due priority to the development of friendly relations with the countries of South Asia. India's foreign policy towards South Asia has been driven by two motives: consolidating and strengthening its position in the region and effectively checking the intervention of super powers in the settlement of regional problems.

These two factors necessitated the foreign policy establishment to keep the neighbouring countries within its sphere of influence and to establish its commanding position at the regional level. This has often lead to a widespread belief among the members of South Asia that India had the real intention of expansionism, which according to some is 'proto-imperialism' i.e., an imperialism in the process of formation or 'sub-imperialism' i.e., an imperialism in the process of formation, but yet subordinated to another imperialism (D.N., 1988). Realising the fact that the tough stand on various issues taken at the regional level will lead to weaker states to rally behind the global powers and with their aid raises controversial regional disputes on various regional and international forums, India from the early 1980s began to strengthen its relations with South Asian states. But there is an intense debate as to whether India has a regional policy at all.

One of the main reasons for the absence of effective regional multilateralism in South Asia is India's South Asian policy. Despite its effective argument for multilateralism in global affairs, India has always followed bilateralism in its relations with South Asian neighbours (Sahasrabuddhe, 2003). Since its Independence in 1947, India has been following *"carrot and stick'* policy while dealing with small powers of

South Asia. In the name of co-operation, she has followed a repressive and suppressive policy and has flexed its military might on the relatively smaller countries in the region and also provided concessions to those who fall in line with her actions. India's big brother attitude has therefore, created much apprehension among her neighbours.

However, the ideologues of Indian state, while stressing that India's 'pre-eminence' in the region must be recognised, try to portray India's role as a benevolent one, one which rescues the neighbouring countries from the mechanisations of imperialism and even contribute to the development of the countries (D.N., 1988). The difference of opinion on the issue of India's role in the region is another reason for the belated start of regional multilateralism. When Bangladesh, for the first time, took the initiative for forming a regional co-operative organisation, India has been very sceptical as it thought that such an organisation would provide a common platform for her neighbour against India, which would ultimately lead to the regionalization of bilateral dispute.

The relationship between India and Pakistan manifest a high level of trust deficit. Two aspect of India's foreign policy based on its national interest are often misinterpreted by South Asian neighbours, especially Pakistan. First, India is concerned about its autonomous status in the region. Autonomy for India requires that the whole South Asian region be free from outside influences. Second, contrary to her neighbour's perception, India has vital interest in the territorial integrity, sovereignty and independence of all the South Asian countries. Thus, Indian foreign policy makers seek to maintain the status quo and consider Pakistan as the irredentist power in the Kashmir dispute (Das, 1996). India is still relying on military security as an instrument to fulfil her regional aspirations. The problem of Kashmir has given the ruling elite, both in India and Pakistan the excuse to engage in hostile arms race and deflect their attention from the most pressing problems they need to address (The Hindu, 2014). They have been using it effectively for securing their political ends.

The size of the economy and geo-strategic position has given India a unique advantage in shaping the political economy of South Asia. The success of regional integration depends upon the extent of trade initiatives adopted by India since she is the largest trading partner in the region. However, India's foreign policy failed to tap the economic potential of the region due to the lack of political commitments. India failed to comprehend the hard realities of contemporary international economic environment.

Despite the fact that the success of India's economic liberalisation programmes depends on the ability to find new markets, both regionally and globally, she has been giving importance only to regions outside the sub-continent. But there are two reasons that make South Asia's trade with new markets outside the region less attractive. Firstly, the world economy is currently expressing a weak growth and is likely to grow more slowly in the coming years also, which make South Asian countries to expand their exports rapidly. Second, with the formation of regional economic blocs and growing protectionism in developed and developing regions, South Asian countries may find it difficult to gain access to these markets (Kishor, 1996).

Therefore, the best possible alternative is to encourage the process of economic co-operation at the regional level. India's foreign policy should recognise this and take additional responsibility in ensuring the participation of all nations in the region.

India's bilateral trade with individual SAARC countries reveals that there is a favourable balance of trade for India despite the fact that during 2012-2013, it has witnessed a negative growth rate of exports with Sri Lanka, Afghanistan, and Maldives. The continuing negative balance of trade for other South Asian countries reveals that they had to transfer some of their hard currency earnings to India which in turn could hardly foster their development but subordinate their development to the requirement of the Indian state. Thus, the complementary relationship between India and other South Asian economies ties these economies into a colonial relationship by making them suppliers of primary products and buyers of Indian made manufacturers. Moreover, some of them serve as additional sources of cheap labour.

The quantum of trade between two great economies, India and Pakistan is also very low compared to other small economies of the region (Table 6.4). This low level of interaction between two economies is due to their prioritization of political conflict over economic gains. Political priorities often overpower economic logic in trade negotiation. Political conflict between the two countries is the greatest hurdle which prevents the whole region from integrating, progressing and prospering. Continued tension between India and Pakistan will only fuel extremist religious forces in both countries, to the detriment of their economy and polity (Hussain, 2010).

Table 6.4: India's Bilateral Trade with Pakistan

(US$ million)

Year	Export	Import	Total Trade	Balance of Trade
2006-07	1350.09	323.62	1673.71	+1026.47
2007-08	1950.53	287.97	2238.5	+1662.56
2008-09	1439.88	370.17	1810.05	+1069.71
2009-10	1573.32	275.94	1849.26	+1297.38
2010-11	2039.53	332.51	2372.05	+1707.02
2011-12	1541.56	397.66	1939.21	+1143.9
2012-13	2064.79	541.87	2606.66	+1522.92

At the base of the conflict lies several issues, but the memory of traumatic and bloody partition, the continuing dispute over Kashmir, and the alleged sponsoring of jihadi groups have played a decisive part in determining their relationship (Naz, 2012). The non-tariff barriers are very high between these two countries as a result of political negativism. If any country, India or Pakistan does not want to trade in some goods, the non-tariff on those products will be increased. Due to these issues the neighbouring states remained reluctant to invest in strengthening bilateral trade ties. The adversarial relations between the two states, therefore, impact the development potential of the entire region, preventing technical efficiencies, better resource allocation and specialization in production (Naz, Ibid).

Even though there is increasing scope for economic integration, the foreign policy establishment in India has been under a dilemma in finding the right direction of her engagement with South Asia. India's foreign policy is caught between New Delhi's aspirations for regional security management and its inability to legitimate those aspirations on the basis of a region-wide consensus (Ayoob, 1990). Any measures aimed at securing greater role in the region will be viewed by her neighbour as an act of hegemony and thereby jeopardising the objective of regional co-operation. India's lack of initiative will also be viewed as lack of enthusiasm towards strengthening the SAARC.

Moreover, the dilemma of comprehending India's role in South Asia is a stumbling block towards effective regionalism. India with its military, economic and geographic advantages claims a leadership position, but other regional powers are reluctant to acknowledge it. Therefore, any attempt taken at the regional level seems to be counterproductive: advice is viewed as interference, assistance is viewed as instigation and guidance is viewed as domination (Bhasin, 2013). Despite considerable benefits accruing to regional economies, they still argue that India's effort at improving regional economic co-operation was a mechanism of ensuring the economic development of India at the expense of South Asian neighbours. The smaller countries fear that they will be dominated by a larger neighbour is the single greatest factor impending cooperation in South Asia.

Despite all this factors, Indian foreign policy had done a little in ameliorating the scepticism among the countries of South Asia. She is still following a coercive diplomacy through economic and military power for ensuring compliancy for her actions. This attitude has naturally invited China to engage with the region which poses a serious challenge to the Indian interests. Being a close ally of Pakistan, China has also begun to engage with Bangladesh, Sri Lanka, and Nepal on energy cooperation and economic development. Therefore, India would have to be more innovative in its foreign policy in South Asia and exercise its economic diplomacy and soft power to engage with these countries (Ambikesh, 2012). India has to re-orient her foreign policy within the prism of regional development and stability.

The effective method is to follow a moderate policy i.e. an accommodative diplomacy giving due share to all members of the region. The replacement of suspicion by confidence is the most pressing requirement. By virtue of its size and power, India has the greatest role to play in bringing about an atmosphere of mutual confidence among the states in the region (Tiwari, 1985).

Adoption of such a policy is more conducive in the changed economic and political environment both at the regional and global level in the post-Cold War era. India's foreign policy during the early period was under the conviction that regionalism will not contribute substantially to India's development. But now Indian policy makers realized that it is in India's interest to promote international trade. The success of India's economic liberalisation programmes largely depends upon her ability to increase exports to new markets both in developed and developing economies.

Therefore, while maintaining economic ties with markets outside the region, India can no longer ignore her base in South Asia, where she enjoys a comparative advantage in almost every sector. India's engagement with South Asia will provide an opportunity to convince the world of India's commitment towards maintaining political stability and regional development with SAARC.

Moreover, India's accommodative diplomacy will naturally instil confidence or trust among the members. They will also realize that despite the existence of several bilateral and multilateral political issues between them, intra-regional trade and economics will promote their interest in South Asian countries altogether. The direct trade of various commodities, currently being diverted through a third country, benefit both India and others regional powers in term of time, energy and price. Besides, many goods being imported at high cost from other countries can be made available from India. By importing from India, SAARC countries will be able to save their hard earned foreign currency.

Conclusion

Even though regional multilateralism has been materialized in South Asia with the creation of SAARC, it failed to strengthen regional cohesiveness due to various inter-state political conflicts, in which India's foreign policy have a decisive role. South Asia is highly dominated by a single power, India, not only in terms of territory and population but also in terms of resource and trade. Therefore, regional co-operation and development in South Asia depends on India's active participation and sincere political commitments. India has to redefine its role, from seeking reciprocity in bilateral relations, to being prepared to go the extra mile in meeting the aspirations of other SAARC nations. The recent Government's initiative is a positive direction in this regard. But it seems too early to have a fruitful judgment at this point.

References

Ali, Ershad and Talukder, Dayal (2010), "Political Economy of Preferential Trade Liberalisation and Regionalism in South Asia: Opportunities and Challenges", *Canadian Social Science*, Vol. 6, No. 3, p. 20.

Ayoob, Mohammed (1990), "India in South Asia: The Quest for Regional Predominance", *World Policy Journal*, Vol. 7, No. 1, p. 126.

Bhargavn, K.K., Bongartz and Sobhan, F. (eds.) (1995), "Shaping South Asia's Future: Role of Regional Cooperation", Vikas Publishing House Pvt. Ltd., New Delhi.

Bhashin, Madhavi (2013), "India's Role in South Asia: Perceived

Hegemony or Reluctant Leadership", available at: http://www.globalindiafoundation.org.

Bratersky, M.V. and Lunyov, S.I. (1990), "India at the End of the Century: Transformation into an Asian Power", *Asian Survey*, Vol. 30, No. 10, p. 928.

Chawla, Kanhiya (1991), "Economic Co-operation among Developing Countries with Special Reference to SAARC", RBSA Publishers, Jaipur, p. 1.

Dash, C. Kishor (1996), "The Political Economy of Regional Cooperation in South Asia", *Pacific Affairs*, Vol. 69, No. 2.

Delinic, Tomislav (2011), "SAARC: 25 Years of Regional Integration in South Asia", KAS International Report, p. 9.

Din, Ud Musleh and Nasir, Shabhaz (2005), "The Regional Economic Integration in South Asia: The Way Forward", Vol. 43, No. 4.

Gupta, Anirudha (2000), "Building Democracies in South Asia", *Economic and Political Weekly*, Vol. 35, No. 13, p. 1071.

Gupta, Anirudha (1996), "Issues in South Asia", *International Journal on World Peace*, Vol. 13, No. 4, p. 5.

Hafiz Wasim Akram, Daoud Ciddikie and M. Altaf Khan (2014), "India's Trade Relationship with SAFTA Countries: A Review", *Journal of Indian Research*, Vol. 2, No. 1.

Haider, Zaglur (2001), "Crises of Regional Cooperation in South Asia", *Security Dialogue*, Vol. 32, p. 427.

Hasan, Zubeida (1964), "South Asia as a Region", *Pakistan Horizon*, Vol. 17, No. 2, p. 162.

Hossain, Manir and Duncan, C. Ronald (1998), "The Political Economy of Regionalism in South Asia", Economic Division Working Paper, SA 98/1, National Centre for Development Studies, Australia.

Human Development Report (2014), United Nations Human Development Report.

Hussain, Akmal (2010), "The Challenges and Drivers of Regionalism in South Asia: The India-Pakistan Peace Process", in Rafiq Dossani, Daniel Sneider, Vikram Sood (eds.), 'Does South Asia Exist? Prospects of Regional Integration', Stanford University, Shorenstein APARC, p. 7.

Kher, Priyanka (2012), "Political Economy of Regional Integration in South Asia", Background Paper No. RVC5, UNCTAD.

Kreinin, M.E. and Plummer (1993), "A Reply to Richard Pomfrets

Comments", *World Development,* 21, p. 1439.

Mansfield, D. Edward and Milner, V. Helen (1999), "The New Wave of Regionalism", *International Organizations,* Vol. 53, No. 3, p. 589.

Maskay, Nephil Matangi (2003), "Monetary Cooperation in South Asia: Some Issues", *Economic and Political Weekly,* Vol. 38, No. 51, p. 5343.

Michael, Ardent (2013), "India's Foreign Policy and Regional Multilateralism", Palgrave MacMillan, UK, p. 1.

Naz, Afsheen (2012), "Political Dominance or Economic Gains: A case study of India-Pak Trade and Perceptions of the People of Pakistan", *South Asia Journal of Peace Building,* Vol. 4, No. 2.

Pant, Pradhan and Gartaula (2014), "Regional Cooperation and Integration in South Asia: Nepal's Perspective", 15th Annual SDN Conference, Ghana, p. 2.

Sahasrabuddhe, Uttara (2003), "Paradigm Shift in Indian Foreign Policy", *Indian Journal of Strategic Studies,* October.

Shaheen, Faisal Moeed (2007), "Regional Integration, Trade and Conflict in South Asia", *International Institute of Sustainable Development,* p. 11.

Soderbaum, F., and Granit, J. (2014), "The Political Economy of Regionalism: The Relevance of Inter Waters and the Global Environment Facility", A STAP Issue Paper, Washington, D.C., p. 19.

Tiwari, K. Chitra (1985), "South Asian Regionalism: Problems and Prospects", *Asian Affairs,* Vol. 12, No. 2, p. 19.

Tripathi, Ambikesh Kumar (2012), "Contemporary Challenges to India's Foreign Policy", *International Journal of Social Science and Interdisciplinary Research,* Vol. 1, No. 7, p. 93.

7

India and the Evolving Power Structure in Southeast Asia

Baljit Singh

India consolidated its position in the Southeast Asian region through economic diplomacy that has been supplemented by the naval diplomacy. In the strategic domain, the ASEAN countries are looking towards India not only as a reliable security partner but also as a state having capability to moderate growing Chinese influence in the region. The ASEAN states do have a security threat from China in South China Sea (SCS), whereas, they are looking towards New Delhi as a security opportunity as they believe in the India's naval capabilities to provide the security to Sea Lanes of Communication (SLOCs), which are vital for their economic well-being. India joined the ARF in 1996 and has been conducting joint naval exercises with the navies from the Southeast Asian states at bilateral and multilateral level besides signing the defence pacts and strategic partnership agreements with some Southeast Asian states.

India's strategic partnership with Vietnam and convergence of strategic interests with US, Japan and the ASEAN countries is an important feature of changing strategic space in this region. Such a scenario leads to a series of questions. What type of power structure has been emerging in this region? Whether India, US, Japan and the ASEAN would be able to balance China's assertion in Southeast Asia as latter treats it as its area of influence? What would be India's position in the evolving power structure in the SEA region? In this paper, a modest attempt has been made to explore these and related questions.

Introduction

Southeast Asia and Asia-Pacific region have been occupying prime place in India's foreign policy priorities since 1990s. Hence, New Delhi cannot remain aloof from the power play going on there. Before configuring India in the evolving power structure in Southeast Asia and Asia-Pacific, it is imperative to have an understanding about the material reality prevailing there and New Delhi's stakes it. Prime objective of New Delhi has been to construct the shared economic, strategic and cultural spaces with Southeast Asian region and thereby to realize its immediate goal to expand trade with ASEAN states and the ultimate goal to expand its area of influence in the region falling beyond South Asia and in the Asian continent at large.

Further, from the strategic perspective also, since Beijing has penetrated the South Asian region and has been trying to enter in the India Ocean through its "String of Pearls Policy", it becomes pertinent for India's security. Likewise, Southeast Asia, which China treats vital for its interest, has become critical for New Delhi. It provides India with an opportunity to moderate China's strategic penetration in the Southeast Asian region. However, the hard reality is that a considerable degree of power asymmetry exits between New Delhi and Beijing—as the latter does not appear threatened by the former while India seems to occupy tremendous insecurity confronted by China's rise on its border, in Southeast Asia and Asia at large. Nevertheless, to moderate China's rise is a strategic necessity for New Delhi to retain its status as a regional power and to materialize the status of emerging power in the foreseeable future.

New Delhi's Interests in Southeast Asia

In the neo-liberal era, there has been a paradigm shift in India's economic policy from inward oriented to outward oriented strategy of economic development. In order to ensure economic growth at home, New Delhi started connecting with outside world in which Southeast Asia figured prominently, due to various reasons.

First, the Southeast Asian region has been pioneer in experimenting with the neo-liberal economic policies that resulted in high economic growth rate. New Delhi opted for the neo-liberal economic policies in early 1990s and therefore, it started looking towards the Southeast Asian region as a role model in the success story of neo-liberal policies, notwithstanding the economic crisis the region suffered in late 1990s.

Second, New Delhi's experience of institutionalizing economic linkages with South Asian countries has proved dismal, therefore, it thought of connecting with Southeast Asian region which had emerged not only as a model of economic dynamism but also as a successful model of regional economic cooperation under the aegis of Association of Southeast Asian Nations (ASEAN).

Third, India is having geographic contiguity with this region—as it has been connecting with it not only through the maritime route but also through the continental route, particularly after Myanmar's joining of ASEAN in 1997.

Fourth, New Delhi has cultural linkages with Southeast Asian region—as it has been a land where Buddhism took birth. Due to that, India has been a destination of religious tourism for the people of Southeast Asian states.

Fifth, Southeast Asia lies at the intersection of the world's two most heavily travelled sea lanes. The east-west route connects the Indian and Pacific Oceans while the north-south route links Australia and New Zealand to Northeast Asia (Khalilzad et al., 2001: 35). The Strait of Malacca is significant because more than 50,000 ships pass through it annually, approximately transporting 30 percent of the goods traded in the world. More than 50 percent of India's trade and 80 percent of China's oil needs are imported through the Malacca Strait. Southeast Asia is the entry point for Chinese shipping into the Indian Ocean and Indian shipping into the Western Pacific Ocean (Egberink and Putten, 2011: 33).

Sixth, Southeast Asia has become significant for India because it has emerged as a source of energy and Myanmar is identified as a rich source of oil and having the largest natural gas reserves. According to official estimates, Myanmar has oil reserves of around 600 million barrels, and total gas reserves of 88 trillion cubic feet, only slightly less than Indonesia (Sinha, 2009). Vietnam is considered as another source of oil and gas reserves and ONGC has already explored oil in SCS—as the two oil blocks No. 127 and 128 were contracted out by the Petro-Vietnam.

Strategic Scenario in Southeast Asia and Beyond

The strategic scenario prevailing in Southeast Asian region indicates that China has been an ascending power, the US has been a descending power and India and Japan are yet to be the powers of consequences. Such a scenario has posed a serious challenge to the US position as a dominant power in Southeast Asia, East Asia and Asia Pacific and global power at large. Further, Chinese assertion has already sent an alarming signal of insecurity amongst ASEAN states, East Asian nations in general and the nations engaged in conflict with Beijing in SCS and East China Sea (ECS) in particular. The Southeast Asian states have been trying to moderate China's assertion by enmeshing it in regional forums like ASEAN Regional Forum (ARF) and East Asia Summit (EAS).

Interestingly, the ASEAN has been engaging Beijing to tame the neo-mercantilist realpolitik that has been characterizing China's foreign policy behaviour. However, Beijing has been using the same institutions as an instrument to extend its regional influence and had always tried to exclude others like India and US from the EAS. Moreover, while planning the first East Asia Community (EAC) Summit, China tried to exclude India, Australia and New Zealand, but was overruled by Japan and ASEAN members. As China's regional influence grows, most ASEAN members are working to push against or balance Chinese power (Schmidt, 2008: 40). The People's Republic of China

(PRC) has been using these multilateral forums to expand its influence in Southeast Asia and East Asia and promote an exclusive form of Asian regionalism that suits its hegemony in the Asian continent. The Southeast Asian region appears to have been sandwiched between the Sino-US contestation.

The ASEAN-US and ASEAN-China relationships are intertwined—since close relations between ASEAN and China undermines the US influence in Southeast Asia, while conversely greater American engagement with the ASEAN, limits China's influence. Though, limiting the other's influence in Southeast Asia is a major geo-strategic interest for both the powers (Egberink and Putten, 2011: 33), but to increase its influence in that region is a strategic necessity for New Delhi. However, the recent strategy of United States to 'rebalance' has been designed to carve out a greater role for Washington that has become its utmost strategic necessity to counter the rapidly increasing influence of Beijing in Asia and Asia-Pacific. Besides US, Japan has been also making moves to counter the Chinese assertion. The EAC proposed by Japan to counter China's proposal of an East Asia Free Trade Area (EAFTA), also includes India. Both India and Japan are well aware of China's not so subtle attempts at preventing their rise. Beijing's stance is most clearly reflected in its opposition to the expansion of the United Nations Security Council (UNSC) to include India and Japan as permanent members (Pant, 2013: 8).

Further, it has also posed a serious threat to India's status as a regional power and New Delhi's larger interests in these regions—as Beijing's economic and strategic penetration in these regions has had a major impact on the power structure. Strategic dilemma confronting New Delhi is how to respond to the evolving US-China contestation in these regions because Washington has already declared *Pivot of Asia* as a strategy of rebalancing in Asia. However, Beijing does not only want to marginalize US in Southeast Asia and East Asian regions but also wants to reduce the increasing penetration of New Delhi in these regions whereas, Washington wants to augment

India's presence there. In addition to Japan, US wants India to be a part of its rebalance strategy to counter the PRC's influence in the Asian theatre because Beijing is a security threat to New Delhi in South Asian theatre and has been posing a serious threat to its status as a regional power in Southeast and East Asia. Paradoxically, New Delhi's joining as a junior partner in the US strategy of rebalancing Asia would also downplay India's status of a pre-eminent power.

Though to safeguards its interests in Asia region, it is extremely important to balance China as a rising power-as both New Delhi and Beijing are competing to expand their influence in the developing world and especially in Southeast Asia. Another paradox of New Delhi is that if it keeps itself away from power play going on in Southeast Asia, as it amounts to giving more leverage to Beijing and thereby undermining its status as a regional power. New Delhi had already experienced that supporting Beijing's case for the permanent seat in the United Nations Security Council and acknowledging the PRC's claim on Tibet by forfeiting its own rights in Tibet, did neither earn China's goodwill nor generate political capital between the two Asian giants. Rather it resulted into Sino-Indian war in 1962 resulting in substantive loss of territory to Beijing.

Moreover, the PRC's recent incursions on Sino-Indian border and its warning to India on oil exploration in SCS are already bothering New Delhi. The dilemma of New Delhi is that if it does not counter Beijing's moves in Southeast Asia, it jeopardizes its regional power status and if it counters PRC's assertion then it amounts to dragging itself in a conflict that has already been taking shape amongst China and ASEAN states (like Vietnam and Philippines), US and Japan in Southeast and East Asian theatre. Although, India's economic and strategic linkages with Southeast and East Asian nations have grown significantly during the last two and half decades yet compared to Beijing, New Delhi is less influential in Southeast Asia despite the fact that the latter enjoys more goodwill than the former—as the PRC has emerged as a security threat to some members of ASEAN and East Asian nations. India is a security opportunity and is a benign power for them whereas the PRC is hostile and a hegemonic power for them.

As Zhang Guihong admitted, "an emerging India does mean a strong competitor for China from South, West, Southeast and Central Asia to Indian and Pacific Oceans where their interests and influences will clash" (Guihong, 2005: 289). India's strategic interests are in clash with those of the Beijing in its extended neighbourhood including Southeast Asia and the Indian Ocean region.

However, India's interests are to counter the domination of economic and strategic space by the PRC in Southeast Asia and East Asia but its concerns in the Indian Ocean have been threefold: to deter hostile powers from operating against India, to maintain Sea Lanes of Communications (SLOCs) for general trade and particularly energy supplies, and to project its power (Scott, 2009: 114) in the larger Indian Ocean region. Japan is also reassessing its role as a security provider in the region and beyond. India seems most willing to acknowledge Japan's centrality in shaping the evolving Asia-Pacific security architecture. While China's rise figures in the evolution of Indo-Japanese ties, so too does the US attempt to build India into a major balancer in the region. In addition, India has committed itself to provide a stable supply of rare-earth minerals to Japan, a clear response to China's reported informal blockade of the strategic minerals after the Senkaku standoff (Pant, 2013: 7).

Evolving Power Structure and Options for New Delhi

New Delhi has confronted with three diverse strategic scenarios from Southeast Asian, East Asian regions and beyond. First, the ASEAN Regional Forum (ARF) was formed in 1994 to promote the regional security cooperation which has brought the states with widely diverging strategic perceptions and priorities under one umbrella. Main objective of ARF has been to engage regional and global players apart from the members of ASEAN in a meaningful strategic dialogue in the SEA and Asia-Pacific region, and to avoid strategic competition and conflict in this region. It also aimed at ensuring that the strategic space in this region should not be dominated by any one country. Its purpose was to create shared strategic space in the SEA region by engaging the states of diverse strategic priorities in a common security dialogue.

The ARF was designed to ensure absence of conflict amongst the major players; to encourage cooperation amongst the major powers towards SEA and to achieve a balance of interests and influence amongst the major players, so that the strategic space in the region should not be monopolized by any single power. Intention was to keep the US in the region and also to bring in the rising powers and socialize them into the habits of peaceful cooperation and confidence building. Through the instrument of ARF, the ASEAN was trying to ensure the peaceful rise of new powers like China, India and Russia while balancing them with a continued US presence. In the process, it was also discouraging the US from trying any containment of the rising powers, in particular of China, while encouraging the new powers to conduct themselves according to universally accepted international rules (Singh, 2010: 21).

Second, the rise of China and its assertion in the Southeast Asia demonstrates that the evolving power structure in the region is taking the hegemonic shape. The United States because of its pre-occupation elsewhere particularly in the Middle East and Afghanistan and increasing economic interdependence between the US and Chinese economies, did not take keen interest in Southeast Asia from 1990 to 2010. That provided Beijing with an opportunity to consolidate its position in Southeast and East Asian regions. The Obama Administration tried to pursue a policy of cooperative strategic engagement towards the PRC and tried to construct a strategic partnership under the assumption that Beijing wants to operate within the international order—as Washington and Beijing shared the same threats ranging from terrorism to economic instability and nuclear proliferation. Further, the US Secretary of State, Hillary Clinton, suggested that the multi-polar world would be multi-partner world where Washington could use its unique global role to foster cooperation among major powers for collective benefit.

Moreover, the Obama Administration went all out to woo Beijing—Obama refused to meet Dalai Lama and did not raise the issue of human rights while visiting China in 2010; postponed the decision to sell arms to Taiwan and downgraded India in America's strategic calculus. However, the PRC read it as a symbol of US decline and saw it an opportunity to assert itself as never before (Pant, 2011: 10). But this did not happen as China attempted to establish its hegemony in the region. Increasing China's assertion to shape regional order not only in SEA and East Asia but also in Asia-Pacific and Asian order at large and the US response thereof, indicated that the agenda and objectives of ARF are relegated to the background as the strategic space therein was going to be more competitive, contested and at times conflictual rather than cooperative.

Third, threatened by the increasing Chinese assertion in the SCS, the Southeast Asian states again started looking towards their old benefactor the US and new friend India to deal with China in strategic realm. Consequently, the US started taking keen interest in Southeast Asia's most intractable territorial dispute in SCS. The dispute in SCS is not merely about resources, it is also central to China's ambitions for blue water navy able to operate away from its shores (Ibid). It appears that China's growing domination in the region would not go unchallenged. Despite growing Chinese influence, the US continues to retain a dominating position in SEA. The US-ASEAN Enhanced Partnership Agreement of 2005 seeking closer cooperation in trade, investment and security is a step towards ensuring greater involvement in the region. ASEAN too seeks enhanced US cooperation to obviate overdependence on China. India's emergence is seen as positive development by the

Asia-Pacific nations (Dwivedi, 2011: 11).

Further, it can be argued that India's first and the most suitable option was to work within the cooperative security framework under the aegis of ARF and ASEAN at the centre and other stakeholders ranging from China to India on board, but it did not work. Second option characterized by the PRC's domination in the strategic landscape of Southeast and East Asia did not suit India's interest because both Beijing and New Delhi were competing for influence and resources in the Southeast Asian, East Asian, Asia-Pacific regions and Asia at large. Moreover, Beijing did not want New Delhi to expand its influence in these regions, as their economic and strategic interests clash with each other. However, the third option that had placed Washington at the centre of structure power of Southeast Asian, East Asian and Asia-Pacific regions did not suit New Delhi's interests in the absolute sense of the term. Because New Delhi walking along with Washington in these regions may help to tame the PRC's assertion but it is bound to have reflections on India's status as a regional power aspiring to be an emerging power.

India's Strategy in Southeast Asia

New Delhi has been evolving and diversifying its strategy to secure its interests in Southeast Asia, East Asia and Asia-Pacific regions. India's *Look East Policy* (LEP) of 1992 has been the first significant step in this direction. Initially, India has used LEP to construct shared economic space between New Delhi and ASEAN states. In this process, India has travelled a long journey ranging from sectoral dialogue partnership of ASEAN (1992) to ASEAN-India Free Trade Agreement (FTA) in Services and Investment (2014). India and ASEAN had crossed many milestones during the last two and half decade including full dialogue partnership, India-ASEAN Summit level partnership and India-ASEAN Free Trade Agreement in goods. The increasing volume of trade between India and ASEAN further speaks about expanding shared economic space between the two partners. Apart from constructing the shared economic space through multilateral channel, India and ASEAN nations have also attempted to expand shared economic space at bilateral level by signing the free trade agreements.

Naval Diplomacy

Besides economic diplomacy, India and ASEAN have also constructed shared strategic space between themselves through the instrument of ASEAN Regional Forum (ARF). India's joining of ARF (1996) has brought ASEAN on its strategic orbit. Being a full-fledged member of ARF, India has become part of the security dialogue of ASEAN. India's membership of East Asia Summit (EAS) has further expanded strategic space for New Delhi in the ASEAN and East Asian regions. However, China opposed India's inclusion in EAS but ASEAN and Japan insisted for New Delhi's membership of EAS—as it was required to make strategic space more inclusive in these regions. Apart from being part of multilateral security forums like ARF and EAS, India has extensively used naval diplomacy to construct the shared strategic space with ASEAN—since the medium of connection between the two is Indian Ocean in general and the Bay of Bengal in particular. Indian navy in diplomatic and benign contexts has been exemplified by the joint exercises and joint patrolling of the sea gates and choke points which has been indicated in the MILAN exercises off the Andaman Islands—headquarters of the Andaman and Nicobar Tri-service command (Prabhakar, 2009: 235).

India's navy has already become a prominent instrument of New Delhi's 'Look East' projection, with naval diplomacy appearing to be more cost-effective. India started the biennial MILAN naval exercise with Southeast States in 1995 with five states including India, Indonesia, Singapore, Sri Lanka and Thailand. However, the number of states participating in MILAN has increased from five to seventeen over the period of time. The MILAN exercises have been conducted nine times, in 1995, 1997, 1999, 2003, 2006, 2008, 2010, 2012 and 2014. The Indian navy hosted the ninth edition of the biennial MILAN exercises for six days in Andaman Sea in February 2014. The MILAN 2014 was the biggest and unique as the countries from western Indian Ocean Region also participated including two African nations viz. Kenya and Tanzania besides the participation of Island nations of Maldives, Mauritius and Seychelles. Philippines and Cambodia participated for the first time. The participation of Southeast Asian navies in India's Bay of Bengal MILAN exercises is being increasingly reciprocated by India's naval deployment in Southeast Asian waters (Scott, 2009: 122).

David Scott argued that India's maritime power projection in the eastern reaches of the Indian Ocean was witnessed in the form of the dispatch of a powerful naval group, consisting of *INS Viraat* accompanied by the guided missile destroyers *INS Rajput* and *INS Ranjit*, the indigenously built missile corvette *INS Khukri* and the replenishment tanker *INS Shakti*. These were deployed at Singapore, Port Kelang in Malaysia and Jakarta in Indonesia during July and August 2005 (Ibid., pp. 122-123). Many more naval group dispatches followed this apart from the goodwill port visits by the naval ships. Since 1993, India has been conducting joint naval exercises with the Republic of Singapore navy named as SIMBEX and most of these joint exercises have been held in the Andaman Sea in the Bay of Bengal which resulted in Indian deployment in the Strait of Malacca and further east into China's backyard of the SCS in 2005 and 2009. The 21st series of SIMBEX hosted by India was conducted from May 22-28, 2014. Improvement in India's maritime relations with Indonesia and Vietnam has expanded its naval presence in the eastern waters.

It is not surprising that various Indian commentators like Anindya Batabyal see such Indian projection in Southeast Asia as an attempt by India to balance China (Batabyal, 2006). Since 2002, navies of India and Indonesia have been carrying out coordinated patrolling twice a year. The 24th edition of

India-Indonesia Coordinated Patrol (CORPAT) was conducted from September 9-30, 2014. Apart from conducting multilateral and bilateral naval exercises with ASEAN states, India has also been conducting joint naval exercises with Japan and the United States. India's growing strategic partnership with Japan has facilitated its entry into Japanese waters, where passage exercises were conducted with Japanese navy in October 2008 in the East China Sea (Chellancy, 2007).

The MALABAR was a bilateral naval exercise between India and US which was set in motion in 1992. It has transformed from a bilateral to trilateral naval exercise. At various points, Indian warships carried out joint naval manoeuvres with the US navy off Okinawa as part of the MALABAR 2007 exercises, rendezvoused off Vladivostok with the Russian fleet as part of the INDRA 2007 exercises, and carried out further trilateral exercises with Japanese and American naval forces off the Japanese coast (Scott, 2009: 125).

This was indeed a long distance maritime diplomacy, a trilateral format repeated in April 2009 in the MALABAR exercises off Okinawa which also reflected India's "rising ambitions with an eye on China" in the Asia-Pacific (Pant, 2007). Such trends have meant that India is becoming a "Pacific player", at least in the western Pacific reaches (Scott, 2007). The 18th edition of MALABAR naval exercise started on July 24, 2014 in the Pacific Ocean. The navies of India, US and Japan took part in this naval exercise.

India's efforts to make itself relevant to the region comes at a time of great turmoil in the Asian strategic landscape. Recent developments have underlined China's aggressive stance towards US allies in Southeast Asia, and there may be more tension to come. Empowered by its economic and political rise, the PRC has attempted to dictate the boundaries of acceptable behaviour to its neighbours. Consequently, regional states have already started reassessing their strategies, and a loose anti-Beijing balancing coalition is emerging. New

Delhi's role becomes critical in such an evolving balance of power (Pant, 2013: 5). As Singapore's elder statesman Lee Kuan Yew has argued, he would like India to be "part of the Southeast Asia balance of power" and "a counterweight to Beijing in the Indian Ocean" (Suryanarayana, 2011). Japan feels that the Indian Navy is the only regional force that can be trusted to secure Indian Ocean sea-lanes that are vital for Japan's energy security. It is also important for India to join hands with the much larger Japanese Navy, Asia's most powerful, to make sure that no adversarial power controls the regional waterways (Pant, 2013: 7).

Further, India's defence relations with South Korea have assumed significance due to the changing balance of power in the Asia-Pacific region—South Korea is a leading country in naval shipbuilding technology and New Delhi needs Seoul's help to augment its own naval capabilities. Besides this, they have a larger interest in protecting the sea-lanes of communication in the India Ocean region (Ibid., 9).

Vietnam has emerged a critical component of New Delhi's strategy towards Southeast Asia—as Hanoi has always supported a leading role for New Delhi not only in Southeast Asian theatre but also at the global level. Growing convergence between New Delhi and Hanoi has enabled India to build Vietnam as a strategic pressure point against China. India and Vietnam's growing strategic partnership with United States further augmented their capabilities to deal with the PRC. To cement their strategic partnership, Vietnam has granted India access to the port of Nha Trang, strategically located near the naval base at Cam Ranh Bay. Moreover, India and Malaysia have decided to work together to secure the Malacca Straits, and the latter has requested New Delhi's help in protecting the Straits from non-traditional security threats in the region. China's claims over the Spratly Islands have further remained as a source of anxiety for Malaysia (Ibid., 12).

Beijing has been unsettled due to the emerging strategic equation between New Delhi and Washington in the Southeast Asia, Asia-Pacific and Indian Ocean region. New Delhi and

Washington have cautioned Beijing to avoid the use of force and abide by the United Nations Convention on the Law of Sea in its maritime disputes with South Korea, Japan, Taiwan, Vietnam, the Philippines, Brunei, Malaysia and Indonesia. On US President Barack Obama's visit to India from January 25-27, 2015, China's State-run media had stated that India must not fall into the trap of rivalry set by the West to support the US' "pivot to Asia", strategy mainly devised to counter the PRC's rise. While reacting to China's reaction, President Obama stated that "I was surprised when I heard that the Chinese government had put out these statements…China does not need to be threatened because we have good relations with India".

President Obama, however, cautioned the communist giant against bullying small nations such as Vietnam or the Philippines on maritime issues. He further said, "my belief is that in this moment in history, there's an opportunity to create a win-win formula in which all countries are abiding by the common set of rules and standards and we are focused on lifting up prosperity for our people, not at the expense of others, but together with each other. That's what my discussions with Prime Minister Modi have focused on". He opined that he had continuously emphasized that it was very much in the US interest to see a peaceful rise of China (The Tribune, 2015: 18).

With China building deep-water ports to its west and east and a preponderance of Chinese arms sales going to Indian Ocean states, India fears being encircled by China unless it expands its own sphere of influence. The two countries' overlapping commercial and political interests are fostering competition, and even more so in the naval realm than on land (Kaplan, 2009: 22). The PRC has already adopted a "string of pearls" strategy in the Indian Ocean that consists of setting up a series of ports in friendly countries along the ocean's northern seaboard. India has responded to China's building of a naval base in Gwadar by further developing one of its own, that in Karwar, India, south of Goa (Ibid., 23). Meanwhile, Zhang Ming, a Chinese naval analyst, has warned that the 244 islands that from India's Andaman and Nicobar archipelago could be used like a "metal chain" to block the Western entrance to the Strait of Malacca, on which China so desperately depends. According to Zhang, India is perhaps China's most realistic strategic adversary (Ibid).

New Delhi's Dilemma

The failure of ARF to construct the shared strategic space and the PRC's increasing assertion in Southeast Asian region has created the fertile ground for a pro-active role of Washington in the strategic theatre of Southeast Asia, East Asia and Asia-Pacific. Obama Administration rolled out the policy of "rebalance" in 2011-12 with more emphasis on military initiatives in the region. Beijing reacted to that by demonstrating its power in maritime territorial disputes with US allies—the Philippines and Japan. In late 2012, it was adjusted by playing down the emphasis on military initiatives and placing more emphasis on its economic and diplomatic efforts and calling for Washington's closer engagement with Beijing (Robert et al., 2013: 7). India has welcomed the US policy to rebalance in Asia but has been cautious to publically embrace the new initiative because it remains wary of provoking Beijing in the light of the widening gap in the economic and military capabilities between the two countries apart from the ongoing border disputes (Ibid., 25).

Moreover, India's historical aversion to alliance-building has led its political establishment to avoid entering into any comprehensive strategic partnership thus far, despite US Secretary of Defense Leon Panetta's description of India as a "linchpin" of rebalance (Panetta, 2012). In response, the Indian Defence Minister A.K. Antony cautioned that the multilateral security architecture in the Asia-Pacific has to be strengthened at a "pace comfortable to all countries concerned" (Antony, 2012). But more than that, the dilemma of New Delhi is that if it is a part of the US strategy of rebalance in SEA and EA and the Asia-Pacific region, it undermines its credential to be power of consequences which New Delhi has been aspiring since the last few years. India being a part of the US strategy in Southeast Asia and Asia-Pacific amounts to being relegated as a subordinate partner like Japan, South Korea and Australia which would dwarf its status as a regional player.

However, to consolidate its position in the strategic and economic theatre of Southeast Asia, East Asia and Asia-Pacific either by moderating or curtailing the PRC's assertion, the million dollar question is that can New Delhi do that on its own. Harsh V. Pant argues that India is emerging as a critical balancer in Asia-Pacific and regional states are recognizing New Delhi's growing clout but India's desires to effectively balance China would remain just a desire without American support (Pant, 2011:10). India's strategic community with realist orientation has recognized that the United State's rebalance strategy for Asia presents a geopolitical opportunity for India—as C. Raja Mohan is of the opinion that the rebalance could compel China "to be more reasonable towards India as China begins to focus on the US military challenge from the east". For instance, following a categorical US commitment to back India for Asia Pacific Economic Cooperation (APEC) membership, China has indicated that it will not be an obstacle on this score (Parthasarathy, 2015: 8).

Conclusion

To sum up, it can be stated that the prevailing material reality indicates the remote possibility of the emergence of inclusive power structure in Southeast Asia and Asia-Pacific region. Beijing has been trying to establish hegemonic power structure there during the last two and half decades and the US recent strategy of rebalance in Asia-Pacific theatre has sharpened the strategic angularities amongst the major stakeholders. Due to that, India has been facing a real time challenge in Southeast Asian theatre to retain its regional power status. New Delhi has already been taking position on the critical issue of SCS confronting the Southeast Asian strategic theatre. However, it needs a lot to do to augment its capabilities to achieve its larger strategic objectives in the ASEAN and Asia-Pacific regions.

Apart from improving its hard power capabilities, New Delhi has already entered into strategic partnerships with Vietnam, Japan, US and other states of Southeast Asia, East Asia and Asia-Pacific regions. India's preferred strategy in Southeast Asia is not to confront China and not to be part of US strategy of rebalance in Asia-Pacific but to strengthen its position in the large Southeast Asian and Asia-Pacific theatre. However, the inevitability of contestation and confrontation with the PRC cannot be ruled out.

Notwithstanding the US strategy to rebalance in Southeast Asia and Asia-Pacific theatre, Washington still wants to bring Beijing in loop provided that the latter respects the rights of concerned Southeast Asian in SCS and Japan in ECS according to the international laws of sea. In this context, the possibility of evolving a bipolar power structure between the US and the PRC in Southeast Asian and Asia-Pacific theatres cannot be ruled out but the presence of other stakeholders like ASEAN, Japan and India in the strategic domain of Southeast Asia and East Asia may be instrumental in shaping the multi-polar and inclusive power structure in Southeast Asia and Asia-Pacific. The latter suits the interest of India, Japan and ASEAN at large whereas the former is more suitable to the interests of Washington and Beijing.

References

Antony, A.K. (2013), Defence Minister, Government of India cited in Ollapally, Deepa M., "India's Response to the US Rebalance", in Sutter, Robert G. et al., "Balancing Acts: The US Rebalance and Asia-Pacific Stability", Elliott School of International Affairs and Sigur Center for Asian Studies, The George Washington University, August.

Batabyal, Anindya (2006), "Balancing China in Asia: A Realist

Assessment of India's Look East Strategy", *China Report*, Vol. 42, No. 2, pp. 179-197.

Chellancey, Brahma (2007), "Japan, India: Natural Allies", *Japan Times*, August 16.

Dwivedi, G.G. (2011), "Checkmating the Dragon's Growing Influence", *The Tribune*, July 6.

Egberink Fenna and Frans-Paul van der Putten (2011), "ASEAN, China's Rise and Geopolitical Stability in Asia", *Clingendael Paper No. 2*, Netherlands Institute of International Relations, Clingendael, April, pp. 1-55.

Guihong, Zhang (2005), "US-India Strategic Partnership: Implications for China", *International Studies*, Vol. 42, Nos. 3-4, pp. 277-293.

Kaplan, Robert D. (2009), "Centre Stage for Twenty-First Century: Power Plays in the Indian Ocean", *Foreign Affairs*, Vol. 88, No. 2, March-April, pp. 16-32.

Khalilzad, Zalmay et al. (2001), "The United States and Asia: Towards a New U.S. Strategy and Force Posture", monograph, Santa Monica. CA: RAND, pp. 1-277.

Mohan, C. Raja (2013), cited in Ollapally, Deepa M., "India's Response to the US Rebalance", in Sutter, Robert G. and et al., "Balancing Acts: The US Rebalance and Asia-Pacific Stability", Elliott School of International Affairs and Sigur Center for Asian Studies, The George Washington University, August.

Obama Barrack (2015), "China Mustn't Feel Wary of Indo-US Ties, says Obama", *The Tribune*, February 3.

Pant, Harsh V. (2007), "India in the Asia-Pacific: Rising Ambitions with an Eye on China", *Asia-Pacific Review*, Vol. 14, No. 1, pp. 54-71.

—-(2011), "Asia-Pacific Strategic Landscape: India Must Make Use of Opportunities", *The Tribune*, November 23.

—-(2013), "China Rises, India Ponders: India's 'Look East' Policy Gathers Momentum", *The Fearless Nadia Occasional Papers on India-Australia Relations*, Vol. 1, Spring, pp. 1-18.

Parthasarathy, G. (2015), "Concern Combined with Realism: China Unsettled by the Readiness of the US and India to Expand their Military Ties", *The Tribune*, February 12.

Prabhakar, W. Lawrence S. (2009), "Maritime Security Triangulation of ASEAN-Australia-India: An Indian Perspective", William T. Tow and Chin Kin Wah (eds.), 'ASEAN-India-Australia:

Towards Closer Engagement in a New Asia', Singapore: Institute of East Asian Studies, pp. 219-242.

Schmidt, J.D. (2008), "China's Soft Power Diplomacy in Southeast Asia", *Copenhagen Journal of Asian Studies*, Vol. 26, No. 1, pp. 22-49.

Scott, David (2007), "Strategic Imperatives of India as an Emerging Player in Pacific Asia", *International Studies*, Vol. 44, No. 2, pp. 123-140.

—-(2009), "India's 'Extended Neighbourhood' Concept: Power Projection for a Rising Power", *India Review*, Vol. 8, No. 2, pp. 107-143.

Singh, Daljit (2010), "The Major Powers and South East Asian Security", K.V. Kesavan and Daljit Singh (eds.), 'South and Southeast Asia: Responding to Changing Geo-Political and Security Challenges', New Delhi: Knowledge World, pp. 13-28.

Sinha, Tuli (2009), "China-Myanmar Energy Engagements, Challenges and Opportunities for India", No. 134, December, *IPCF Issue Brief*, The Institute of Peace and Conflict Studies (IPCS), New Delhi, pp. 1-4.

Sutter, Robert G. et al. (2013), "Balancing Acts: The US Rebalance and Asia-Pacific Stability", Elliott School of International Affairs and Sigur Center for Asian Studies, The George Washington University, August, pp. 1-53.

U.S. Department of Defence (2012), "Panetta Says US-India Relations Must Deepen, Grow for Peace", New Delhi, India, June 6.

8

India's Prospects in BRICS

Shubhi Misra

It is quite evident that there is a shift in the balance of power from a unipolar to a multipolar world. The emerging power blocs are becoming an object of concern for the traditional powers. The factors that determine the status of states as weak or strong are many but in contemporary times it is the balance between the economics and politics which is crucial. The present trend in global order clearly demonstrates that the developing countries are coming to the forefront and rapidly advancing in the league where they could if not challenge but compete with the global pre-eminence of the West. It was the financial crisis of 2008 in which G20 gained prominence in the world. It was then that the growth pattern of countries such as China and India that came into picture which shocked the world.

The coming up of BRICS nation is not only giving rise to a different world order but it has also come up with a new regionalism. This 'new regionalism' is not based on territorial proximity but can rather be viewed in ideational terms. It is a result of plethora of discursive practices that relies on representation of realities. Regions are not physical entities that remain constant rather they are set into dynamism by changing pattern of association and dissociation in the world. BRICS can also be viewed as a subset of nations who have purposefully come together to realize common economic goals in an integrated collective manner. The construction of geo-economic bloc is the most striking feature of this association. The member countries have a common perception of identities and meanings of the existing actors in the international political realm. The unique synergies of these states has both an element of physical and cultural trait in it. BRICS ventures to create new 'spaces of flow'. [1]

BRICS might not have entirely become institutionalized but it is not an informal arrangement which is directed towards achieving short-term desired collective goals. The current pace of advancement in its working has catered attention from all directions—gradually with further growth and passage of time the impact and the structural value of this regime shall become clear and unclouded.

The present paper attempts to evaluate BRICS from a critical perspective and appraise how coherent the forum is as a player in the international realm. The coming together of these countries has both geo-economics as well as geo-political underpinnings. The first section of the paper discusses the escalating cooperation between the developing countries where it talks about how individual states are benefited by entering into alliances while the next section talks about BRICS, its upcoming cooperative bank and its reserved funds. China has evolved tremendously and its role in the world and also in the multilateral forum like these cannot be overlooked. The last section of the paper tries to locate India's individual interest amidst the widening scope of BRICS and its bilateral ties with the West.

Multilaterism in South-South Cooperation

After the disintegration of Soviet Union, the IR scholarship was endowed with inputs on multilateralism which continues till today. Multilateralism has gained prominence because in the era of increasing globalisation and dependence, states see the prospects of mutual gains from such alliances. Power dynamics and multilateralism have close link with one another. John Ruggie defined multilateralism as "an institutional form that coordinates relations between three or more states based on generalized principles of conduct, that is, principles that specify the adequate conduct for each type of action, disregarding the particular interests of the parties or the strategic demands that may appear in each case in particular" (Ruggie, 1992: 14).

The extent of multilateral engagements of a state depends on the trade-off between the individual needs of the state to the collective procurements of group activities. States are at times sceptical in their involvements because of the undermining of their individual motive and goals at the cost of the group. There are two main reasons of states' economic and political cooperation—first is the state's individual interest and the second is an exogenous challenge. By entrusting in international institutions and bequeathing of economic powers in them, states practice shared sovereignty.

BRICS

It was in 2001 that economist Jim O' Neill from Goldman Sachs speculated in his paper, 'Building Better Global Economics' about the growing economies of Brazil, Russia, India and China. It was Neill who coined the acronym 'BRIC' for the first time. As predicted by Neill, in the last decade BRIC nations were ranked in the top ten slots of countries with highest GDP in terms of purchasing power parity. BRICS is an association of developing economies that have come together on a common platform to collectively deal with economic issues. Following its inception in 2009, this association has assumed a prominent place in the global political and economic proceedings.

With the inclusion of South Africa in 2010, the association assumed a more pluralistic form. The underlying principle that dominates this grouping is that integrating economies and market related reforms are crucial efforts towards economic stability. Many scholars have criticised this association by labelling it as weak (Tudoroiu, 2012: 24). It cannot be denied that BRICS has a lot more to strive and formalise in its institutional settings to become a strong actor in the international system. It is nascent, evolving and flexible at this early stage but is certainly a potential forum which could possibly have beneficial prospects for these developing countries. An association like this which includes strong regional state actors from different parts of the world is competent to acquire a transnational status.

Taking cues from the foundational theory of IR-realism, it can be exclaimed that the international political system is anarchic in nature. There are insecurities and constant struggle for power among the states. Waltz suggested balance of power to explain the behaviour of states. By evaluating the present structure and arrangement of BRICS from the lens of neo-liberalism, one can arrive at a certain conclusion. First, the member actors are the chief actors and their role cannot be undermined. The states indulge in cost benefit analysis and the coming together on a common platform for mutual cooperation clearly denotes the fact that there lies an individual interest in being a part of the BRICS association.

Generally, the developing economies with large population sizes rely on institutionalized developmental structures to ameliorate themselves vis-à-vis other states (Schmaltz and Ebenau: 2012: 490). Another derived analytical understanding of BRICS reveals that the member states look for absolute gains. The existing trajectory of the growth of China and its economy suggests that it is emerging at a very fast rate and has gained impetus in almost all the spheres. The benefits accrued by China from this association shall possibly be large and in the long-run it is likely to attain its goal of transforming from emerging to a developed state.

BRICS is not only facilitating cooperation but also giving an opportunity to the members to maximize their individual profits. Neo-libral outlook explains that for realising self-interest even the rational egoist actors can cooperate in the given anarchical system.

New Development Bank

The intergovernmental agreement to establish NBD was held at the Fortzela summit in July 2014. NDB is a first step of collective action by the emerging powers. The growing economies of developing countries are in the active process of getting away with their third world status and becoming at par with the developed countries of Europe and North America. The underlying aim with which this bank is established is to provide the member states, security against risks and economic challenges in the global economy. The proposal in the summit reveals that NDB is aimed at providing infrastructural needs with sustainable development at its core. From the perspective of sustainable development diplomacy, it is very essential for the BRICS to formulate their policies that are in tandem with this theme.

With increasing awareness among the nations towards sustainability and environmental protection, it would lie in the benefit if the BRICS strictly adheres to the standard norms. If at all they go against the sustainable development principles there would be an increasing criticism by rest of the countries which is very likely to hamper the growth and progress of BRICS. By recognising that there exists a congenital relation between development and environment it was agreed by all the countries in UNCED that they had the common responsibility to safeguard the global crisis of environmental protection by focussing on sustainability (Papa, Gleason, 2012: 10).

There is no denial of the fact that the southern countries have been left aloof from the global policy making procedures. There are a plethora of forums where these countries do not feature. However in 2010, it was acknowledged by the IMF that the participation of the developing countries does not correspond to their increasing economic influence in the world. As a result, a modest increase of 6 percent quota share was implemented. In general, it is also believed by some that the US dominant institutions tailored them to their larger needs at the stake of less developed countries. The third world countries and BRICS nations in particular have now assumed a revisionist tendency to bring a paradigm shift in the prevailing system. NDB is a first step of collective action by the emerging economies.

There are opinions that NDB might challenge the existing financial institutions while others hold the view that it would rather compliment rather than challenge the credentials of the long established institutions. It is pointless to claim that NDB is formulated with the motive of posing any threat to the Bretton Woods system. The financial set up of Bretton Woods is the first of its kind; it is deeply rooted in the multilevel cooperation of its members. All the members of BRICS are individual members of IMF as well since they have taken indirect or direct assistance from different schemes launched in the organization. The Bretton Woods twins—IMF and World Bank—are successfully operating since 1944 and are huge in their scale both in terms of membership as well as the capital. They have robust financial backing and have comparatively lesser risks in the global market. Given the fact that NDB is in its incipient stage, it is not possible for it to entirely meet their demands.

There exists a gap between the finances required to the finances needed and to bridge these gaps, it is a requisite for BRICS to maintain benign relations with the IMF and the World Bank. In the Summit, it was also proposed to include developed nations as minority stakeholders with an aim to increase the credit rating thereby helping it raise more funds. It is likely that the developed countries would extend their willingness in being a part of NDB. Such an investment opportunity would give the developed world some influence in this association. It is definite that once the bank takes a formal footing it would surely work at expanding its membership. At this stage it is required that there is co-financing from public and private enterprises to this financial structure.

Contingency Reserve Agreement (CRA)

The Fortzela Summit also put forth a joint monetary fund CRA. The member countries have decided on a US$ 100 billion contingency fund, which they can draw on in financial emergencies when their foreign exchange reserves become dangerously depleted. CRA would give cushion against external pressures. It would also be used to tackle short-term liquidity pressures that impede economic growth. The recent market analysis shows a bit unfavourable trend for the developing world. There is a decreasing tendency in the price of the commodities (such as the decrease in the crude oil price). Since India ranks third in terms of oil imports, it is benefited domestically, while China that has a huge amount invested in liquid stock market is likely to be adversely affected by the descending commodity rates. Foreseeing these economic upheavals, the market analysts and investors are shifting towards those economies that depend on more stable currencies such as dollar.

The BRICS countries currently have the world's largest foreign currency reserves, and the new institution offers an opportunity to invest those savings at a profit. China contributed US$ 41 billion to the capital stock; India, Brazil and Russia each paid in US$ 18 billion and South Africa's share was US$ 5 billion. Apart from these, the forum has decided to follow one nation one vote norm. The equal voting share would surely ensure uniformity and equality in terms of participation. In order to ensure greater participation and involvement in decision-making, the group has decided to have the provision of rotation in presidents. The project is a positive venture and holds great promises for the developing nations; however it is very crucial that various schemes under BRICS and NDB in particular, should undergo rigorous evaluation and adopt professional approach. There has to be transparency in the dealings and proper coordination between the local development banks and the NDB.

The domestic imperatives associated with these five countries are many including the prevailing corruption at the domestic level might affect this project as well. Another challenge for NDB is raising of such huge funds—the accruing of the proposed funds is likely to take considerable time.

While calling for investment from other countries and the expansionist bend of the association, it is important to contemplate with the democratic set up as proposed under BRICS—would it confine to the member countries alone or it will extend to other investors also. The elaborate schemes and goals of BRICS and NBD can be fruitful only if they do not replicate the existing hegemony prevailing in institutions and rather include equity, transparency and inclusiveness in their approach.

Recently at the G-20 finance ministers' meet held in South Korea in January 2015, the US and European nations came up with the proposal of 'bank tax'. Many developing countries including the BRICS strongly condemned the proposal. The unexpected proposition of bank tax was indirectly hinting at the fact that there is some insecurity in the Western world about the upcoming of NDB.

China's Preponderance

The expansion of Chinese economy and its rapid pace of growth and development have brought China in global limelight. It is actively engaged in redefining the global economic structure. China is behaving rationally and the Chinese strategy can be broadly classified under two broad frames. First, it is engaged in building a strong infrastructure and acquiring self-sufficiency by focussing on economic activities, military capabilities and technological innovations and so on. Second, it is venturing into collaboration and alliances with other states to compete with the established powers. It is also adopting flexi-powers that include amalgamation of both soft as well as hard and is continuously engaged in increasing its influence on a global level by establishing SEZs (special economic zones).

Among BRICS, China's performance is many times better than the other member nations. This brings to forefront a major issue of concern; will China assume a dominant role in BRICS, directing the course and becoming hegemonic. At many occasions it is opined, 'that is China's position in BRICS akin to United States' status in Bretton Woods institution'. Various analogies are drawn between BRICS and the World Bank. The main thrust out of which BRICS was conceptualized is the dissent of a strong influence of powerful nations like US in the decision-making of the international institutions. China's increasing supremacy has built scepticism in scholars, policy analysts and also to an extent in member states of BRICS. From India's outlook and owing to its inter-state relations with China, it becomes complicated and difficult to adjust with a political dilemma like these. Owing to changes such as establishment of development bank, economic activation of the developing world and so on, some scholars have expressed that 'Beijing Consensus' is the new replacement for 'Washington Consensus' (Babb, 2012: 18).

India's Broader Foreign Policy

With changing global scenario and increasing dependence, the policy of non-alignment has become redundant for India. In order to establish itself globally, India has always been focussing on strengthening its policies and strategies. The high GDP has projected the country as one of the strong contenders of major global power. It can be seen that India has adopted a very flexible and area\issue specific foreign policies and diversification while approaching disparate problems. With the implementation of new economic policy in 1991, India had opened a gateway of transactions for itself. The impact of this economic revision affected foreign policy too. By looking at the trajectory of India's policy it can be deduced that India has amalgamated different approaches in IR. At the international level, we can observe that it is guided by the principles of multilateralism, at the inter-state level it is making use of selective bilateralism and it is also entering into group activities by indulging in selective coalition (Wulf and Debiel, 2015: 30).

For greater participation and involvement in international

organizations, the policy of multilateralism has been adopted by New Delhi. There has been a long standing demand by India for a permanent seat in UNSC (United Nation Security Council), and an increasing share of voting rights in other institutions. The US continues to play the diplomatic games with the underlying hegemonic intentions masked in multilateralism. Few scholars assert that "in relation to developing countries, multilateralism has become a decisive tool, for its normative and institutional framework, channelled through the United Nations' system or private regional organizations" (Mino and Olmedo, 2013: 71). India actively got involved in multilateral pursuits owing to the international competition as a means to establish itself in the inter-state networking. It also adopted this policy with a view of making use of multilateral ties as a defence against parallel unilateralism.

BRICS broadly shall affect the members in two ways: first is the economic consequence, and the second is political outcomes. For all stakeholders, the economic advantages shall be more or less on similar lines but the political implications are country specific and shall vary across the spectrum. Economically it shall provide prospects to expand their respective capitals, build infrastructures and promote inclusive growth. The larger question about BRICS grouping is, 'will the BRICS forum give India an opportunity to realise its foreign policy objectives'. The elaborate proposals and policy under BRICS and NDB is now put to real test. The further advancements in working of the bank shall make the scenario clearer as to how far is the clubbing of the five countries successful and how much are the individual gains. At this juncture, it is difficult to predict the consequences of the bank and the contingency funds but India will surely have to be certain of its manoeuvring keeping in mind its long-term foreign policy and global interests.

In spite of a strong bilateral trade and collective involvement of India and China on various common forums, their inter-state relations are not perfectly cordial. There have been issues regarding the territorial disputes and border interpretations. Between 2010 and 2012, there were almost 550 instances of Chinese encroachment in the Indian territory (Times of India, September 2012). China has also meddled in highly volatile areas of Jammu & Kashmir by deploying Chinese soldiers in PoK (Pakistan occupied Kashmir). Further, the infrastructural endeavours of China in the disputed Aksai Chin area by building Xingjiang-Tibetan highway have also exacerbated the inter-state dynamics. The Arunachal Pradesh province of India is referred by China as Southern Tibet and people of that region were issued stapled visa.

Another area where the two states came against each other was the South China Sea—China strongly condemned India's oil exploration projects in the Sea. China diplomatically masks its offence as defence and India has experienced duplicity in Chinese dealings on a number of occasions. The deception in Chinese political transactions has compelled India to be cautious at every step. The prodigious project under BRICS and China's active role makes India sceptical on all levels. India has to foresighted in assessing China's activity and it has to acquire a prominent position in making BRICS and its allied schemes transparent with equal decision-making rights of the member countries.

A decade ago, the rapid growth of China had become a major concern for the United States. As a result of which there emerged a competitive culture between the two nations. Chinese expansion and its developing market gained momentum after the US suffered from the global financial crisis of 2008. In 2009, the trade deficit of the US fell to nearly 3 percent of its GDP, while Chinese economy was soaring high at the same time. Chinese goods dominated the global market—even the advanced and developed countries could not escape from them. Chinese intention became very clear which was not viewed to be benign by the developed world, US in particular. Once again there is some scope of tables turning, with the IMF's speculation that American growth in 2015 is expected to be 3.6 percent faster than the collective economy of the entire world (The Indian Express, January 19, 2015).

In 2010, the Chinese currency grew 10 percent more than the US dollar while it is now slipping again. It is quite evident that the American economy is resuming back and this shall certainly affect the market dynamics globally. If such trends persist then there shall be growing dependence on American economy which will prove fatal for China. The current pattern suggests that Chinese exports are beginning to show a downward trend, the falling of renminbi is very likely to give impetus to serious structural reforms and deepening reliance of the world on American economy. China is engaging in rebalancing techniques by focusing on those services that would give heavy returns thereby giving a further boost to its economy.

As far as India is concerned, for it, both America as well as China is an important global player and it lies in India's benefit to strike a balance between the two. The relations between India and US are taking a new shape specially after the signing of the nuclear deal in 2005. There have been a series of visits from both the sides that had a positive impact on the inter-state relations. In September 2013, the then Prime Minister Dr. Manmohan Singh and in 2014 the present Prime Minister Narendra Modi also visited US following which US president Obama was invited on India's Republic Day. The visits emphasised on improvement in the relations between the two countries. For India, the civil nuclear agreement and ensuing energy security is of vital importance. Despite such collaborated efforts, both from the Sino-China and US-India side, New Delhi has remained apprehensive about foreign policy of either of these states.

Conclusion

The significance of any congregation or association such as BRICS is determined by the power of various kinds. It is not only the collective or absolute power of the individual stakeholders but also how other actors in the international sphere perceive it and evaluate it in terms of power. NDB is an initiative that is not only notable but the democratic set up within which the bank is formed makes it distinct as well. However, the future course of the bank's working progress and realization of the proposed goals shall be the actual determining factor of the evaluation of NDB. It shall be imperative to assess whether the bank is truly and practically the bank of 'New World Order'. There are other spheres like investments, funding and other infrastructure related issues that are still to be properly materialized. As soon as these institutional and infrastructural procedures are sorted, the bank would begin building its foundation. There is a lot of scepticism regarding the growing influence of China and its hegemonic intent in the working of the bank, but the other member states and their proactive involvement in the group shall not give room for any lopsidedness to appear.

With 'Make in India' campaign of Prime Minister Narendra Modi, it is clear that the country is poised to go ahead in the direction of greater connectivity, industrialisation and economic restructuring with more foreign direct investment. At this juncture, it is very crucial to see the future course of the bank and also how well the Government of India is able to make use of this opportunity in realizing its individual dreams.

Endnote

1. It was Manuel Castells (1996) who defined the concept of place space and spaces of flow. According to Castells space of flow 'is the material organization of the time-sharing social practices that work through flows and networks (Castells, 1996: 412).

References

Aggarwal, Raj (2012), "Outward Foreign Direct Investments by the BRICS", *Journal of Teaching in International Business,* pp. 314-316.

Andreasson, Stefan (2011), "Africa's Prospects and South Africa's Leadership: Potential in the Emerging Market Century", *Third World Quaterly,* pp. 1165-1181.

Babb, Sarah (2012), "The Washington Consensus as Transnational Policy Paradigm: Its Origins, Trajectory and Likely Successors", *Review of International Political Economy,* pp. 1-30.

Craig, Kern (2010), "The New World Order: A Deconstruction of the Nation-State and a Disaggregation of the Mixed Political Economy", *International Journal of Public Administration,* pp. 414-420.

Debiel, Herbert Wulf and Tebias (2015), "India's Strategic Autonomy and the Club Model of Global Governance: Why the Indian BRICS Engagement Warrants a Less Ambiguous Foreign Policy Doctrine", *Strategic Analysis,* pp. 27-43.

Ebenau, Stefan Schmalz and Matthias (2012), "After Neoliberalism? Brazil, India, and China in the Global Economic Crisis", *Globalizations,* pp. 487-501.

Ferchen, Matt (2012), "Whose China Model is it Anyway? The Contentious Search for Consensus", *Reviw of International Political Economy,* pp. 1-31.

Griffith-Jones, Stephany (2014), "A BRICS Development Bank: A Dream Coming True?",

Hui Fang Cheng, Margarida Gutierrez, Arvind Mahajan, Yochanan Shachmurove and Manuchehr Shahrokhi (2007), "A Future Global Economy to be Built by BRICS", *Global Finance Journal,* pp. 143-156.

Jones, Andrew F. Hart and Bruce D. (2011), "How Do Rising Powers Rise?", *Global Politics and Strategy,* pp. 63-88.

Kappel, Robert (2011), "The Decline of Europe and the US: Shifts in the World Economy and in Global Politics".

Kim, Kap-Young Jeong and Euysung (2010), "The Global Financial Crisis: New Implications and Perspectives for Emerging Economies", *Global Economic Review: Perspectives on East Asian,* pp. 1-13.

Legro, Jeffrey W. (2012), "The Politics of the New Global Architecture: The United States and India", *Strategic Analysis,* pp. 640-644.

Malone, Rohan Mukherjee and David M. (2011), "From High Ground to High Table: The Evolution of Indian Multilateralism", *Global Governance,* pp. 311-329.

Mihaela, Papa and Nancy W. Gleason (2012), "Major Emerging Powers in Sustainable Development Diplomacy: Assessing their Leadership Potential", *Global Environmental Change*, pp. 1-10.

Miño, Paloma González (2014), "State and Multilateralism, A Theoretical Approach: Transformation in a Globalized International Society", Janus.Net *e-Journal of International Studies*, pp. 69-83.

Panda, Jagannath P. (2012), "A 'BRICS' Wall? The Complexity of China-India Multilateral Politics", *Indian Foreign Affairs Journal*, pp. 175-194.

Schoeman, Maxi (2011), "Of BRICs and Mortar: The Growing Relations between Africa and the Global South", *The International Spectator: Italian Journal of International Affairs*, pp. 33-51.

Stephen, Matthew D. (2012), "Rising Regional Powers and International Institutions: The Foreign Policy Orientations of India, Brazil and South Africa", *Global Society*, pp. 289-309.

Timothy, M. Shaw, Andrew F. Cooper and Agata Antkiewicz (2007), "Global and/or Regional Development at the Start of the 21st Century? China, India and South Africa", *Third World Quarterly*, pp. 1255-1270.

Timothy, M. Shaw, Andrew F. Cooper and Gregory T. Chin (2009), "Emerging Powers and Africa: Implications for\from the Global Governance", *Politikon: South African Journal of Political Studies*, pp. 27-44.

Tudoroiu, Theodor (2012), "Conceptualizing BRICS: OPEC as a Mirror", *Asian Journal of Political Science*, pp. 23-45.

Wright, David and Shorr, Thomas (2010), "Forum: The G20 and Global: Goverance and Exchange", *Survival: Global Politics and Strategy*, pp. 181-198.

9

China's 'New *Tianxia*' Strategy and the Indian Response

Jabin T. Jacob

Following the ascension of a new leadership at the 18th CPC Congress in 2012, China has conducted a dynamic foreign policy—on the one hand asserting itself on territorial issues from the East and South China Seas to Line of Actual Control with India and on the other, coming up with new initiatives to draw the Asian continent first and then further field into an ever closer economic and political relationship with China. It is this latter aspect that is the subject of this paper. Two parts of this form of Chinese foreign policy are examined—one, China's frequent hosting of international conferences and seminars and two, its promotion of new ideas and new organizations as a way of shaping a common narrative for Asia with China in the lead.

Alongside, this paper also highlights how India lags behind China in terms of organizing principles and institutional capabilities. By way of conclusion, I suggest that China is harking back to ancient principles and the worldviews of an imperial power as a framework for its foreign policy that continues to evolve in a world where its economic power is growing stronger, the influence of the West appears to be declining and calls for China to take greater international responsibility are also increasing.

China's Conference Diplomacy

In a roughly 30-day period beginning late October 2014, China hosted a major international military dialogue called the

Xiangshan Forum designed as rival to the annual Shangri La Dialogue of the International Institute of Strategic Studies, London (China Military Online, 2014b), the World Internet Conference (Bloomberg Business, 2014), the Fourth Foreign Ministerial Conference of the Istanbul Process on Afghanistan (MOFA, PRC, 2014), a UN meeting on the role of geospatial information in promoting sustainable development (Xinhuanet, 2014f) as well as an international conference each on humanitarian rules governing military operations (China Military Online, 2014a), and anti-hijacking (Xinhuanet, 2014d). In addition, the Chinese government offered to host an informal defence ministers' conference of all ASEAN countries in 2015 (Chan, 2015), and was the designated host of the G20 summit in 2016 (Xinhuanet, 2014e).

Together, these give us a sample of the literally hundreds of meetings of international organizations and associations that China hosts round the year in addition to the normal bilateral meetings involving heads of state and other government officials. Add to these, are the regular conferences that China has begun organizing on its new Silk Road initiatives all across the country where dozens of participants from Asia and around the world participate (for instance, see Xinhauanet, 2014a).

The point about this long list of conferences and events hosted by China is to underline the fact that there are several kinds of diplomatic outreach and China well understands the value of reaching out as often as possible through conferences and seminars to foreign intellectual and policy elites and of ensuring that these elites carry away positive impressions of China. This then feeds into larger policy and diplomatic successes for China at the regional and global levels. Beijing has even begun identifying and inviting those of younger generations who are potentially future thought and policy leaders in their countries.

Indian Prime Minister Narendra Modi has logged thousands of international miles since he assumed office. He has met all the major world leaders, addressed the UN General

Assembly, even gone as far as tiny Fiji as well as completed a circuit of the strategically located Indian Ocean island states of Mauritius, Seychelles and Sri Lanka. He has hosted all the SAARC leaders at home for his swearing-in as well as the Chinese, Russian and American presidents. Modi's schedule and indeed, that of his Foreign Minister, Sushma Swaraj, and her deputy, Gen. V.K. Singh (retd.), might stand out in comparison with those of their counterparts in the previous UPA regime but what the NDA government is doing is merely bringing India up to speed.

India is a country with difficult neighbours and an economy that has not yet found a sustainable pattern of growth and development but it is also simultaneously one that needs to be an active regional and global player in order to defend its national interests. Modi and his ministers will thus have a lot more foreign trips to make and leaders and summits to host if they are to discharge their responsibilities fully.

However, since neither the Prime Minister, nor even the Foreign Minister, can travel everywhere and all the time, they will need greater support at home. There are several problems here, however of limited intellectual resources, of poor infrastructure and of short-sighted bureaucracy and red tape.

One, the Indian government needs an able and well-oiled establishment where diplomats, military officials and scholars work in tandem to both provide analyses and ideas as well as to implement national objectives but there is, at the moment, no such establishment or coordination. And worse, even the intellectual and human resources are lacking. India's area studies programmes are hopelessly under-funded and even experts can barely speak the language of the countries or regions they are studying.

The tiny size of the Indian Foreign Service (IFS) is both a joke and source of frustration among embassies in New Delhi. The IFS is an island with the Indian civil services unwilling to take on lateral entry of specialists whether from other government services or from academia. It also tends to function largely under the illusion that diplomacy can be hived off from the wider strategic community, including academics, as and when they think fit. The Ministry of External Affairs (MEA) has also hitherto been rather close-minded with respect to the role that the armed forces can play in achieving India's wider diplomatic goals, objecting to or plain preventing the armed forces from their equally important attempts at military diplomacy. Given that the IFS lacks the numbers, the military with its pyramidical hierarchy could also provide a great number of perfectly qualified and experienced officers to take on diplomatic tasks across the globe with a little more training.

There is a still more serious issue, namely, India's lack of adequate numbers of qualified foreign language speakers. Most Indians have a preference still for European languages like French or Spanish but not many actually realize that the greatest numbers of French and Spanish speakers actually reside not in France or Spain but in Africa and Latin America respectively. These regions are where the very literatures of these languages are being reshaped and where economies are beginning to grow rapidly. And yet, very few Indian scholars and students or tourists and diplomats actually wish to study, travel or be posted in these regions.

The Chinese, on the other hand, understand that the centre of global growth and dynamism is shifting to these Third World continents and are sending their students, tourists, and diplomats out in large numbers to build a foundation for economic cooperation and political friendship and as a way of promoting Chinese models of political and economic development.

And what of India's near neighbourhood? Despite the threat of terrorism and Islamic fundamentalism originating in Pakistan and in West Asia, despite several nuclear weapons programmes in the neighbourhood, very few Indians in responsible positions actually speak Arabic or Persian or Pashto. Even here, China has made an entry with Chinese oil companies and weapons manufacturers becoming extremely active and the recent appointment of a Special Envoy for West Asia also indicating China's increasing political interest in the region.

While India has close historical ties with Central Asia, including political friendship in more recent times, there are very few Indians who actually speak Turkish or any of the Central Asian languages, surely both a security and political necessity? (for IFS figures, see MEA, GOI, 2014b: 239). If Indian security forces—the three armed services and the intelligence establishments—do not have officers trained in these languages, and not just translators and a few diplomats, it is unlikely that New Delhi ever be able to take initiative in these regions that India is dependent on for its energy security and with their rapidly evolving politics and security situations.

Prime Minister Modi's desire to convert 'Look East' to 'Act East' (MEA, GOI, 2014a) will fail if India does not have adequate numbers of diplomats, military officers, and businessmen who speak the major languages of the region—Chinese, Japanese, Korean, Bahasa Indonesia, Malay or Thai. Despite the long and close ties with Vietnam, Indian government officials who can speak Vietnamese probably number in the single digits (for IFS figures, see MEA, GOI, 2014b: 239). These facts speak for themselves as to the seriousness or lack thereof of India's engagement with these countries and regions.

At major international forums, officials from many of the smaller countries—as well as China for that matter—all prefer to speak in their own languages. How then, for example, can India organize a major international military dialogue like the Xiangshan Forum in China, a G20 summit or any large-scale international conference for that matter with its requirements for simultaneous interpreters for officers and officials from various countries? Chinese capabilities in this regard are truly astounding as is evident at any major event they organize where there are both liaison officers speaking different foreign languages and simultaneous interpretation during conference sessions that range from competent to excellent.

Two, despite its image as a rising power and before that for several decades as a leader of the Third World, India simply lacks the physical infrastructure to host conferences and foreign delegations anywhere beyond the big cities. And sometimes even the major cities fall short in terms of proper transport infrastructure, and adequate numbers of good quality and affordable hotel rooms. The last factor is, in fact, a major hassle and expense for organizations wishing to host events in India with the result that non-governmental conferences often do not have too many participants in order to keep within budget. Hotel rooms in Chinese cities on the other hand are abundant, clean, well-maintained and relatively cheaper.

Whereas in India the 1951 and 1982 Asian Games and the 2010 Commonwealth Games were all hosted in New Delhi, over a two year period from 2008 to 2010, China hosted the Olympics in Beijing, the World Expo in Shanghai and the Asian Games in Guangzhou. China has used major international events to build up infrastructure not just in its capital but in other major cities as well. Even tiny South Korea has hosted the Asian Games in three different locations. [1]

Three, India's default policy of making visas for conference participation or research purposes extremely difficult to get is actually illogical and short-sighted. The Chinese, by contrast, realize the value of interacting with international intellectual and policy elites as often as possible in order to learn what is going on in the world around them, what views of China they hold and to create opportunities to counter or disprove negative views, if any.

By keeping out scholars trying to learn more about India, New Delhi also loses a chance of influencing them and if anything, solidifies negative opinions or misperceptions about India. Of course, China keeps out those scholars who are openly sympathetic to or supportive of say Tibetan independence or Ugyhur separatism but these are the exceptions that prove the rule—the vast majority of scholars and researchers are welcome in China and free to travel and speak at academic and research and government institutions in China.

Confidence, organization and a practically permanent cadre of educated young Chinese to act as liaison officers round the clock for international conference participants arriving in the country—all of these add to considerable propaganda value and goodwill for China. India's poor record of safety for international tourists, of organization of major events—the organization of the 2010 Commonwealth Games in New Delhi, for instance was marred by poor planning and corruption scandals—and poorly-trained human resources, on the other hand, offer a stark contrast. For India to catch up with China will take time but to begin the process, mindsets need to change immediately and the investments in area studies and foreign languages in the universities, in think-tanks and research institutions and in the expansion of the foreign service need to start today.

China's New Initiatives

Since coming to power, Communist Party of China (CPC) General Secretary and Chinese President, Xi Jinping, has not only converted himself into a strongman at home by his tough anti-corruption crackdown, he has also encouraged and promoted innovation in China's foreign policy outreach. One such is 'one belt, one road' (OBOR) initiative launched in 2013. The 'one belt' refers to the Silk Road Economic Belt (*sichouzhilu jingjidai*) connecting China with Central Asia and onwards to Europe while the 'one road' is the 21st Century Maritime Silk Road Initiative (*ershiyi shiji haishang sichouzhilu*) connecting China via the seas to Southeast Asia, South Asia and Africa. These 'new Silk Roads' recall a history when China was an important player in the politics and commerce of the Asian region and to reinterpret this for contemporary times in such a way that both American dominance is countered and other countries accept the centrality and importance of China regionally and globally.

All along these new Silk Roads, China is pushing a mantra it has long believed in, that economic development is a panacea for political instability and disaffection. This involves in the main investment in physical infrastructure development—involving roads, railways, telecom, electricity and energy—alongside encouraging people-to-people contacts in the form of educational exchanges and sister-city agreements. [2] The latter might, in fact, largely be about lubricating big-ticket deals in the countries that lie along the Silk Roads. Whatever, the kind of monies and the diplomatic attention that Beijing is lavishing on its immediate neighbourhood and the countries along the OBOR—many of them small countries, often weak and underdeveloped and which do not receive much attention from the West or its economic and financial institutions—has truly won Beijing a great deal of attention and goodwill, at least among political elites in these countries.

There might be a shadow of sorts hanging over Chinese largesse given the way these are disbursed sometimes with political elites or certain sections among them cornering them or profiting from them in many instances and thus, creating resentment among ordinary people in these countries against China. But the Chinese have some experience of such blowback in many countries including, in Africa, and perhaps that is also why they also lay great stress on people-to-people contacts, the offering of scholarships and why Chinese media is actively involved in literally creating positive stories about China's relations with the country in question as well as of the OBOR. [3] This then contributes to creating a narrative about China that it both directs and benefits from. Essentially, China claims that policies such as the OBOR seek to spread the bounties of Chinese economic growth and prosperity to its neighbours and that this is proof of its intention of peaceful development in the international system.

Another example of the nimbleness and innovation of

Chinese foreign policy is its push to create new institutions as rivals to existing institutions or to fill gaps that have been left unfilled by the dominant Western powers and regimes. Alongside the unveiling of the OBOR, China also created a US$ 40 billion Silk Road Fund (SRF) targeted at specifically the countries that lie along the proposed new Silk Roads (Zhang, 2014). Another initiative that is larger and more inclusive is the Asian Infrastructure Investment Bank (AIIB). This initiative also supports the Silk Roads policy of course, and along with the SRF, stresses strong internal drivers of China's external policy. In essence, the OBOR and its spin-offs—the SRF and to an extent the AIIB—are about exporting the huge overcapacity of Chinese infrastructure companies abroad where many countries actually need this capacity. In the process, China also hopefully avoids further addition to the property bubble and bad debt problems at home, among other things.

Of course, even if China has declared the SRF and AIIB as open to capitalization from other countries, it appears obvious for the moment that China will supply the bulk of the capital—it has promised to fund half of the US$ 50 billion start-up capital for the AIIB (Kemp, 2014)—and therefore, also provide the leadership. Unlike the BRICS New Development Bank, where the first presidency has been allotted to India, but where China insisted on hosting the Bank (Bloomberg TV, 2014), in the case of the AIIB, both the secretary-general and the headquarters are Chinese (The Indian Express, 2014).

While not openly linked to the OBOR, the AIIB also creates foreign policy opportunities for China. It has the opportunity to be seen as both a responsible international stakeholder and a generous partner for countries in the region. Beijing has simultaneously tried to show that its initiatives are not threatening to the existing international order. [4] Besides promoting regional connectivity and self-reliance for Asian countries, the OBOR and AIIB also create opportunities for developed countries in the form of greater investment opportunities as well as for promoting their own economic recovery (China Daily USA, 2014).

As the Chinese Finance Minister Lou Jiwei has pointed out, historically, the establishment of regional multilateral development banks such as the Asian Development Bank (ADB) or the European Bank for Reconstruction and Development did not weaken the influence of existing development banks such as the World Bank. Rather, it was the total capacity of development financing that increased, promoting further development of the global economy. Thus, the AIIB, for instance, will be an additional source for development financing in the Asian region with a specific focus on infrastructure and in contrast to the ADB whose focus is on poverty alleviation (Xinhuanet, 2014b). Lou also stated that the AIIB would learn from the good experiences and practices of other multilateral development banks accumulated over several decades (Xinhuanet, 2014c). This is especially important as Asian nations today, do not have the luxury of repeating the mistakes of the past and must, in fact, enforce even higher standards, in ensuring labour rights and environmental protection, for example. That said, the record of Chinese companies in this respect is not very encouraging whether at home or abroad.

All of these apart, the AIIB has already been the source of great propaganda successes for Beijing given that many nations including India, and in a shock to the United States, even the United Kingdom, signed on as founding members of the AIIB (Snell, 2015). Even if not always overtly so, these Chinese initiatives are clearly targeted against American hegemony in the world. And China has managed to push and promote them in a manner that even the existence of territorial disputes has not prevented all of the ASEAN members from being a part of the AIIB (for full list, see AIIB, 2015). Meanwhile, China has also blocked Taiwan from becoming a founding member (Hornby, 2015).

One might ask where is India in all this? India, with its excellent tradition of banking and financial sector regulatory frameworks, [5] is a natural participant and leader in Asia's multilateral initiatives as well as a partner for China in establishing and strengthening new initiatives. But it is far from certain that India thinks of itself in this manner, as having legitimate cause for striving with China, even when the initiative is largely Chinese in nature—one only has to recall the somewhat reluctant acquiescence India gave to becoming a member of the AIIB and the fact that it sent only a bureaucrat and not a minister to the signing ceremony in Beijing (The Indian Express, 2014). This is a problem that has afflicted India for several decades with reluctance to give whole-hearted cooperation to the Bangladesh-China-India-Myanmar (BCIM) regional cooperation forum, even though India is a member and the persistent attempts to deny China full membership of the South Asian Association for Regional Cooperation (SAARC).

India has shown some signals of greater receptivity to the BCIM in the form of an acceptance of a Chinese proposal for a BCIM Economic Corridor (MEA, GoI, 2012), for example, but this is not proof enough yet that New Delhi has come to the realization that resentment over China's role and abilities to drive regional organization or attempts to keep China out of South Asia are both fruitless exercises in the long-run. While India was part of the first batch of 21 founding members of the AIIB, unlike in the case of the BRICS New Development Bank, where an Indian official is slated to be the first head (NDTV, 2014), Beijing has not been so easily amenable to sharing AIIB's leadership or as of now, giving India much of a say in the organization.

What is more, if the AIIB really takes off—and its members include Brazil, Russia and South Africa—it is unclear what role the BRICS 'New Development Bank' will actually play. It could well be that the BRICS New Development Bank with its equal contributions from the five members but its unwieldy power balance is simply the cover for Beijing to achieve more substantial outcomes through the AIIB which it might more or less control both in terms of capital investment as well as through developing country allies.

Naturally, India's present capabilities and resources do not allow the expression of any great ambition in these matters but the question is whether New Delhi realizes the consequences of the Chinese new initiatives and their drive to create institutions also helps shape the political and economic narrative of Asia in ways that might sideline India as just one among many countries in Asia led by China.

China has spotted and taken advantage of a crying need for infrastructure development and financing and at the same time managed to sell itself as a benevolent power in the region looking out for common interest and 'win-win'. This despite the fact that China has not relented in its assertiveness on the East China Sea and South China Sea disputes and in its challenges to Western interpretations and foundations of international law. Can India stand by and only challenge China from a distance by simply reiterating the need for respecting international law without also say, supporting smaller disputants with its own capacity in international law? Why for instance, when the Chinese have refused to accept international arbitration on their maritime disputes does India not actively advertise, as a sign of how great powers behave, its acceptance of an international tribunal's verdict on a maritime dispute with Bangladesh? [6]

New *Tianxia* and the Challenge for India

Taken together, China's specific foreign policy initiatives—both the nuts-and-bolts version that is the organization and hosting of conferences as well as the grand ideas version of creating new narratives and new organizations as justifications or platforms for Chinese foreign policy activism alongside its assertiveness in territorial disputes constitute a framework of Chinese foreign policy that might be best described as a new form of *tianxia*—or 'all under heaven'—an ancient term that in material, non-metaphysical context, was a framework used by successive Chinese imperial rulers to refer to China's overlordship, including cultural and economic superiority, over neighbouring kingdoms and its prominent role in arbitrating disputes and conflicts between them. [7]

China's organization of conferences at home involving many foreign participants and its drive to create new multilateral institutions are exercises in power—soft and hard. Beijing is attempting to not just increase China's influence but also to put forward a new way of doing business different from the Western/American approaches and trying constantly to assuage fears of Chinese hegemony. To this end, China is beginning to ramp up its engagement with its neighbours in the form of summits, conferences, military diplomacy, infrastructure development and other kinds of investments, media outreach and larger embassies. China's massive financial resources and the attraction of its model of development are on full display through its conferences.

To call Iranians and Saudis together or Indians and Pakistanis, to let them have a go at each other at these conferences or to call Central Asians and Russians under one roof knowing that they might gang up on China and ready to take it on, to call a few sceptical Europeans and Americans but also just as many who are willing to bat for China [8]—these are signs of a confident power. It reflects a belief that China has the ideas and the financial resources—to influence and change mindsets, to fundamentally alter and shape regional and global geopolitics. And what is more, they are willing and ready to do it using multiple methods—the steady undermining of status quo in the east and the soft, non-confrontational conferences/summitry/wining-and-dining system in areas where attitudes towards China are not so (or not yet) sharply antagonistic or suspicious. This constitutes a new form of Chinese dominance of the world akin to *tianxia.*

India needs to keep reminding the Chinese and other participants—whether in conferences or in multilateral organizations—that India too, was a presence on the ancient Silk Routes and continues to be one along the new Silk Roads. The Silk Route is just a name—coined by a German at that [9]—and should not carry the mistaken impression that it was either Chinese in origin or controlled by the Chinese. In other words, it was also Indian products and ideas that travelled through the Silk Route and Indian influence on the Silk Route through the presence of traders and the spread of Buddhism was not inconsiderable. India ought to take seriously, participation in many of these Chinese initiatives in the form of market expos, inter-university cooperation, joint research projects, scholarship exchanges rather than keeping away out of pique or confusion.

Overall, there is a great deal of goodwill for India among the non-Chinese at both these conferences and in China's wider neighbourhood but if China offers such substantial benefits, it is very hard for anyone to resist and it is even worse when India fails to meet even those obligations it has committed to. The hands-off approach Indian officialdom adopts in promoting Indian soft power, is at best trying to make a virtue out of necessity—India simply does not have enough hands in the MEA and in the missions—and at worst, it is a sign of laziness and/or lack of strategic vision.

The new government in New Delhi has declared an 'Act East' policy to replace the older 'Look East' policy but this appears focused on the economic dimension. It must consider however, whether it should not play a more robust role in the political and security domains and in a visible, active manner. This also involves an ideational element—along the lines of what the Chinese have attempted in creating a concept of 'new Silk Roads' and in the process engendering a reinterpretation of history. India, however, cannot rely on creating a 'new history' like the Chinese are doing papering over the uncomfortable facts or, resort to a parochial, nativist view of history. Rather, an Indian idea must both be universally acceptable and stand out as a moral and ideological improvement on other ideas that have come before—whether Chinese or American—as well as be backed by solid capabilities based on political stability and economic development at home that are respectful of the Constitution.

At the base of all this that India must do, however, lies the fundamental problem of lack of human resources capacity within and outside the Indian government. An expansion in the numbers of India's diplomats accompanied simultaneously by an improvement in their quality as well as in the quality of support that they receive from universities, research institutions and think-tanks is the *sine qua non* for India being able to meet the Chinese challenge.

Endnotes

1. The cities were Seoul (1986), Busan (2002) and Incheon (2014).
2. To take one example, namely Pakistan, see Haider, 2015 and Haider and Haider, 2015.
3. Author's observations from conferences attended in Urumqi, Xinjiang on the Silk Road Economic Belt, June 26-27, 2014 and Quanzhou, Fujian on the 21st Century Maritime Silk Road Initiative, February 11-12, 2015.
4. For instance, China reportedly offered the vice-presidency of the Bank to Japan (Nikkei Asian Review, 2015).
5. For instance, the Securities and Exchange Board of India that regulates the Indian stock market was recently ranked 7th worldwide for investor protection, the highest among the BRICS nations and higher even than many advanced economies such as the US, Japan, France and Germany. Significantly, this was a huge jump from its 21st[t] rank in 2013 (Zee News, 2014).
6. This has already been suggested in an influential Singaporean policy publication (Bateman, 2014).
7. The term has been interpreted in multiple ways by Chinese philosophers and intellectuals as well as statesmen. In the modern era, a *T'ien Hsia Monthly* was published in Republican China but the most prominent of recent interpretations is by Zhao Tingyang. Both the monthly and Zhao's work took broader, cosmopolitan, and therefore, somewhat utopian approaches towards the interpretation of *tianxia*. For more, see China Heritage Quarterly (2009) and Zhang (2010).
8. Author's observations from conferences attended in Urumqi,

Xinjiang on the Silk Road Economic Belt, June 26-27, 2014 and Quanzhou, Fujian on the 21st Century Maritime Silk Road Initiative, February 11-12, 2015.

9. The term 'Silk Road' was originally coined by the German explorer Ferdinand von Richthofen in the late 19th century; less well-known is the fact that his explorations and studies also covered the spread of Buddhism from India into China along these Silk Roads (The Silk Road, 2007).

References

Asian Infrastructure Investment Bank (2015), "Prospective Founding Members", available at: http://aiibank.org/members.html.

Bateman, Sam (2014), "Resolution of Bangladesh-India Maritime Boundary: Model for South China Sea Disputes", *RSIS Commentary*, No. 158, August 7, available at: http://www.rsis.edu.sg/wp-content/uploads/2014/08/CO14158.pdf.

Bloomberg Business (2014), "China Hosts the World Internet Conference", November 20, available at: http://www.bloomberg.com/news/videos/2014-11-20/china-hosts-the-world-internet-conference.

Bloomberg TV (2014), "India Gets First Presidency of the BRICS Bk", July 16, available at: http://www.btvin.com/videos/watch/8003/india-gets-first-presidency-of-the-brics-bk.

Chan, Minnie (2015), "China Offers to Host Conference for ASEAN Defence Ministers", *South China Morning Post,* April 29, available at: http://www.scmp.com/news/china/article/1639210/china-offers-host-conference-asean-defence-ministers.

China Daily USA (2014), "Chinese Finance Minister Says AIIB a Win-win for Each Member", October 24, available at: http://usa.chinadaily.com.cn/business/2014-10/24/content_18799109.htm.

China Heritage Quarterly (2009), "The Heritage of T'ien Hsia, All-Under-Heaven", No. 19, September, available at: http://www.chinaheritagequarterly.org/editorial.php?issue=019.

China Military Online (2014a), "Foreign Officers Study Battlefield Humanitarianism in China", September 23, available at:

http://eng.chinamil.com.cn/news-channels/china-military-news/2014-09/23/content_6150995.htm.

China Military Online (2014b), "Xiangshan Forum 2014", November 20-22, available at: http://eng.mod.gov.cn/SpecialReports/node_46641.htm.

Haider, Irfan (2015), "Details of Agreements Signed during Xi's Visit to Pakistan", *Dawn,* April 20, available at: http://www.dawn.com/news/1177129/details-of-agreements-signed-during-xis-visit-to-pakistan.

Haider, Mateen and Irfan Haider (2015), "Economic Corridor in Focus as Pakistan, China Sign 51 MoU's", *Dawn,* April 20, available at: http://www.dawn.com/news/1177109/economic-corridor-in-focus-as-pakistan-china-sign-51-mous.

Hornby, Lucy (2015), "China Rejects Taiwan as AIIB Founding Member", *Financial Times,* April 13, available at: http://www.ft.com/intl/cms/s/0/46745152-e1b1-11e4-8d5b-00144feab7de.html.

Kemp, John (2014), "China Takes Silk Road to Challenge US Role in Asia", *South China Morning Post,* November 12, available at: http://www.scmp.com/business/economy/article/1637664/china-takes-silk-road-challenge-us-role-asia.

Ministry of External Affairs, Government of India (2012), "India's Look East Policy at the 10th Meeting of the BCIM (Bangladesh, China, India, Myanmar) Cooperation Forum", Speeches and Statements, February 18, available at: http://www.mea.gov.in/Speeches-Statements.htm?dtl/18855/Speech_by_Foreign_secretary_on_Indias_Look_East_Policy_at_the_10th_Meeting_of_the_BCIM_Bangladesh_China_India_Myanmar_Cooperation_Forum.

Ministry of External Affairs, Government of India (2014a), "Prime Minister's remarks at the 9th East Asia Summit", November 13, available at: http://www.mea.gov.in/Speeches-Statements.htm?dtl/24238/Prime_Ministers_remarks_at_the_9th_East_Asia_Summit_Nay_Pyi_Taw_Myanmar.

Ministry of External Affairs, Government of India (2014b), "Annual Report 2014-2015", available at: http://mea.gov.in/Uploads/PublicationDocs/25009_External_Affairs_2014-2015__English_.pdf.

Ministry of Foreign Affairs of the People's Republic of China (2014), "The Fourth Conference of the Istanbul Process on Afghanistan Held in Beijing", November 1, available at: http://www.fmprc.gov.cn/mfa_eng/zxxx_662805/t1207147.shtm.

NDTV (2014), "India to Head BRICS' $100 Billion New Development Bank", July 16, available at: http://www.ndtv.com/article/india/india-to-head-brics-100-billion-new-development-bank-559330.

Nikkei Asian Review (2015), "China Offered Japan No. 2 Post at New Bank", April 15, available at: http://asia.nikkei.com/Japan-Update/China-offered-Japan-No.-2-post-at-new-bank.

Snell, Sabrina (2015), "U.S. Allies Split with Washington, Bank with China", *Financial Times,* March 31, available at: http://www.ft.com/intl/cms/s/0/cd466ddc-cbc7-11e4-aeb5-00144feab7de.html.

The Indian Express (2014), "India, 20 Others Set Up Asian Infrastructure Investment Bank", October 24, available at: http://indianexpress.com/article/business/economy/india-20-others-set-up-asian-infrastructure-investment-bank.

The Silk Road (2007), "Richthofen's Silk Roads: Toward the Archaeology of a Concept", Vol. 5, No. 1, Summer, available at: http://silkroadfoundation.org/newsletter/vol5num1/srjournal_v5n1.pdf.

Xie, Fang (2011), "Rethinking Tianxia", *China Quarterly Heritage,* No. 26, June, available at: http://www.chinaheritagequarterly.org/tien-hsia.php?searchterm=026_tianxia.inc&issue=026.

Xinhauanet (2014a), "One Belt One Road Initiatives Key for Building a Safer Asia", September 25, available at: http://news.xinhuanet.com/english/china/2014-09/25/c_127030026.htm.

Xinhuanet (2014b), "AIIB Complementary to Existing MDBS, Says Chinese Finance Minister", October 24, available at: http://news.xinhuanet.com/english/china/2014-10/24/c_133740270.htm.

Xinhuanet (2014c), "AIIB to Set Up High-standard, Feasible Safeguard Policies, Says Chinese Finance Minister", October 24, available at: http://news.xinhuanet.com/english/china/2014-

10/24/c_133740339.htm.
Xinhuanet (2014d), "China Convenes Int'l Anti-hijack Meeting", October 24, available at: http://news.xinhuanet.com/english/china/2014-10/24/c_133740517.htm.
Xinhuanet (2014e), "China to Host G20 Summit in 2016", November 16, available at: http://news.xinhuanet.com/english/china/2014-11/16/c_133793116.htm.
Xinhuanet (2014f), "High Level Geographical Info Forum Held in Beijing", November 22, available at: http://news.xinhuanet.com/english/china/2014-10/22/c_133735273.htm.
Zee News (2014), "India Ranks 7th on Investor Protection: Ahead of US, Japan", October 29, available at: http://zeenews.india.com/business/news/finance/india-ranks-7th-on-investor-protection-ahead-of-us-japan_110867.html.
Zhang Feng (2010), "The Tianxia System: World Order in a Chinese Utopia", *China Heritage Quarterly,* No. 21, March, available at: http://www.chinaheritagequarterly.org/tien-hsia.php?searchterm=026_tianxia.inc&issue=026.
Zhang Yuzhe (2014), "With New Funds, China Hits a Silk Road Stride", *Caixin Online,* December 3, available at: http://english.caixin.com/2014-12-03/100758419.html.

10

Constraints in Indo-US Relations amidst Growing Bonhomie

Josukutty C.A.

The end of the Cold War has effected dramatic changes in Indo-US relations. These two countries, which were on the opposite sides of global and regional politics suddenly painted themselves as natural and strategic partners with the end of the Cold War. In terms of the range and gamut of joint endeavours, agreements and engagements, the Indo-US relationship is at its peak ever. Foreign policy analysts and the public alike are convincingly optimistic that Indo-US relations are all set to evolve and flourish into a truly strategic partnership in the 21st century. The national and international contexts look quite opportune and congenial for a natural and mutually advantageous relationship.

Despite all these congenialities and favourable contexts, a key feature of Indo-US relations has been the unpredictability characterized by swings between periods of cooperation and antagonism. Nothing is guaranteed in Indo-US relations. The upswings in the relationship have very often been sabotaged by seemingly small irritants. Why this happens? Is this the feature of a truly strategic and natural relationship? Are India and the United States still strange bed fellows unable to realize the objective of cementing a strong geopolitical alliance that advances each other's vital interests? The key argument of the paper is that despite the growing camaraderie between India and the US, there are many fundamental differences that could block and derail the prospects of a prospective strategic relationship. In other words, the hyped relationship falls short of a strategic relationship.

Constraints from the Cold War Era

Historically, Indo-US relationship has been characterized by a number of contradictions and constraints. During the Cold War, despite being democracies, India and the US were virtually on the opposite sides of world politics primarily due to their differing ideological positions and world views. [1] Indian concept of independence in foreign policy, non- alignment, anti-imperialism, multi-polar world and world peace were contrary to the US idea of world hegemony, uni-polar world, military alliances and containment of communism. According to Dennis Kux, the root cause of disagreements between India and the US during the Cold War days was the clash over national security issues of prime significance to each country—for India, the US arming and aligning with Pakistan—India's principal security threat and for the US, India's relationship with the USSR, the major threat to American perceptions of global security and peace. [2]

This clash of interest was visible in the pro-Pakistan position of the US on the Kashmir issue, Pak-US military alliances such as the CENTO, US military and economic aid to Pakistan, their joint fight against the Soviet occupation of Afghanistan and in strengthening the China-Pak axis. India adopted a pro-Soviet policy to deal with the security threats it faced from both Pakistan and China with assistance from the US. These differences were so pronounced that they evolved into strategic complications and threatened the stability of South Asia by sharpening the Indo-Pak rivalry. The Indo-Pak war in 1971 brought India virtually on the brink of a direct military confrontation with the US with its naval force moving to the Bay of Bengal in support of Pakistan. These contradictory world views, power asymmetries, national priorities, India's penchant for independence in foreign policy, US's South Asian polices particularly towards Pakistan kept these two eminently democratic countries estranged and on opposite sides of world and regional politics.

New Chemistry in Indo-US Relations

The end of Cold War and the subsequent changes in world politics and India's integration into global economy have reinforced and synergized Indo-US relations at multiple levels. The shift in India's foreign policy was narrated as the convergence of conceptual and strategic understanding with the US. At the conceptual level, leaders of both the countries have evoked, time and again, the significance of democracy as a factor of strategic significance in the relationship. In 1998, Prime Minister Atal Bihari Vajpayee stated that India and the United States, as the world's largest democracies, were "natural allies", a term subsequently used by President Clinton and Bush. [3]

Defending India's nuclear test U.S. Senator Mack emphasized India's commitment to peace and commented, "We have a common bond with the Indian people based on a commitment to democracy, freedom, and the rule of law". [4] The July 18, 2005 joint statement by Indian Prime Minister Manmohan Singh and the U.S. President George W. Bush on the landmark Indo-US civilian nuclear agreement recognized democracy as a guiding principle for building a peaceful, prosperous, inclusive and sustainable world. [5]

In his speech to the US Congress on July 19, 2005, Manmohan Singh said, "there are partnerships based on principle and there are partnerships based on pragmatism. I think we are at the juncture where we can embark on a partnership that can draw both on principle as well as pragmatism". [6] In a testimony before the House International Relations Committee in 2006, Secretary of State Condoleezza Rice stated that the United States has invested heavily in India's rise through economic assistance, defence training and transfer, and civilian-nuclear energy cooperation—to help incorporate India into what she calls "the tent of responsible democracies that wish to be anchors of stability and the promotion of democracy and peace in the world...promotion of democracy and freedom around the world should be an essential component of the new US-India relationship. [7]

The US considers India's identity as a "multi-ethnic, multi-religious and pluralistic" democracy—"the foundation for our partnership in regional and global affairs", while Indian leaders declare "our common commitment to democracy, pluralism, and prosperity"—the basis for Indo-American cooperation on global issues. [8] India and the US are partners in many global democracy promotion endeavours. They became founding members of the Community of Democracies in 1999 and UN Democracy Fund in 2005 to promote representative institutions and human rights worldwide.

On the whole, unlike the Cold War years, democracy has become a common asset of the relationship and has helped India and the US agree and work together internationally at many levels—democracy, market capitalism, rule of law, fighting terrorism, the UN charter and all regimes or webs of international law. [9] Both India and the US support the ideas and principles of 'democratic peace'. A report by the Centre for New American Security says, "The United States and India should work together to spread the culture of democracy in lands where it does not yet exist". [10] In these and other ways, the liberal-democratic identities of America and India have reinforced strategic and economic interests to draw the two nations closer together in an era of uncertainty…and growing threats from failing states and terrorism. [11]

Indian strategists argue that a future balance of power in which democratic India constitutes a principal pole would better protect the liberal values embodied by Indian society than a future order in which an authoritarian China enjoys hegemony in Asia. [12] With the rapid rise of religious fundamentalism and terrorism, both the countries have a common interest in promoting liberalism, political moderation and peaceful change.

The growing ideological affinity has contributed to strengthening of the relationship politically with an explicit pro-US tilt in India's foreign policy. The disintegration of

Soviet Union and the collapse of communism changed the equations of world and regional politics in terms of alignments and realignments. Pakistan lost its strategic significance in the US scheme of things in South Asia. The US was in search of new allies to contain the rise of China. India was found to be the fit candidate to play that role along with the US in South Asia and the Asia-Pacific. According US Defence Secretary Ash Carter, India is "an anchor of global security". [13] The Asian pivot policy considers Indian as a strategic ally along with other US friends in the region. The US shares with India, common objectives regarding Pakistan—a moderate Pakistan that is a responsible nuclear steward, that confronts extremism within its borders and stops supporting terrorism outside of its territory, and that also plays a positive role in maintaining the stability of Afghanistan. [14]

In 2001, India was one of the few countries to support the Nuclear Missile Defence Initiative by the US. The formulation of the Next Step in Strategic Partnership (NSSP) in 2004 and the July 18, 2005 initiative on civilian nuclear cooperation further strengthened the relationship. The Civilian Nuclear Agreement of 2008 and the US-India Strategic Dialogue (annual) that began in June 2010 were manifest of relationship with India as a defining partner in the 21st century. Establishment of the US-India Homeland Security Dialogue in 2011 was also important in improving the relationship.

The elaborate Joint Statement issued at the end of the strategic dialogue in June 2012 said, "The US and India have a shared vision of peace, stability, and prosperity in Asia and joint production and development of defence equipment under the Defence Trade and Technology Initiative (DTTI). [15] The January 2015 joint statement on the Asia-Pacific region further indicated greater commitment of both the nations to collaborate and cooperate in the most vital region of the world today including South East Asia. [16] The Logistics Exchange Memorandum of Agreement signed in August 2016 allows for exchange of logistics support, supplies and services between the two countries' armed forces. [17]

The partnership assumed a comprehensive character that covered economy, energy security, food security, favourable public perception and attitude about each other, dialogues on regional and global issues, strategic dialogue over 100 areas from education to space to preservation of wildlife, strategic talks about different regions of the world, growing economic cooperation, goodwill through diasporas, cooperation on non-proliferation, counter terrorism and defence cooperation, joint efforts in disaster relief, maritime cooperation, nuclear cooperation, high technology and space cooperation. Today, India holds more annual military exercises with the United States than any other country. [18]

Irritants in the Relationship

Despite the tremendous improvements in the relationship, at times, the relationship was held hostage to a number of major and minor incidents. Some of the important issues were the 1998 nuclear test and the US sanctions on India, the diplomatic spat over the Devyani Kobragade incident in December 2013, the disagreements over the Nuclear Liability Bill, dramatic increase in the denial of L-1 (intra-company transfer) and H-1B (temporary work visa) visa for Indian professionals and researchers, disagreements over India's participation in the 70th anniversary of victory day celebrations of Second World War in Russia against US advice, India's unwillingness to commit military responsibilities, India's non-inclusion in the Trans-Pacific Partnership (TPP) and APEC, issues over the visa fee hike for Indian job seekers in the US, Indian complaint on US being mild on India specific terrorists, continued military and economic aid to Pakistan, India's divergence with the US on Syria, Ukraine and Afghanistan.

Differences and Contradictions

Throughout the Cold War, the quest for a strategic partnership between India and the US was frustrated by the two countries' often mismatched worldviews, national priorities, and material capabilities. [19] The current state of Indo-US relationship is truly comprehensive and it covers a wide range of issues and areas. But there are fundamental differences over a number of issues which violate the vital interests of both India and the US. On a number of occasions, they have failed to keep their relationship at a mutually beneficial level. This is visible prominently at three levels—threat to India's fundamental security interests, India's world views and competing economic and political interests.

First of all, there are differences over issues that are of fundamental security interests to India. This includes unhindered US military and economic aid to Pakistan, chinks in the joint fight against terrorism, particularly Pak supported India specific terrorism and, total bypass and avoidance of any collaborative efforts on India's security threats at borders with Pakistan and China. India's most important security threat is from the borders with Pakistan and China. India and US have not so far entered into any treaty agreements to deal with this threat. At the same time, the US has continued with its economic and military aid to Pakistan despite strong opposition from the Indian side. The United States has handed over 14 combat aircraft, 59 military trainer jets and 374 armoured personnel carriers to Pakistan from the weapons it is leaving behind in Afghanistan, reports the Congressional Research Service. [20]

The US State Department has approved Pakistan's request for a billion dollars worth of military hardware and equipment, identifying Pakistan as a country of vital importance for US foreign policy and national interests. [21] The argument is that these weapons are meant to enhance Pakistan's military capabilities to strengthen counter-terrorism and counter-insurgency operations in South Asia. India is the only country against which Pakistan would use the advanced military equipment that it has purchased from the US. It means that the US is supplying weapons to a hostile neighbour of India with whom it has fought four wars and continues to fight a proxy war on a daily basis.

At the same time, the US is very particular on India's collaboration in dealing with the emerging Chinese challenge in the Asia-Pacific through what is called the 'Asian pivot' policy. The US wants India as a partner to protect its geopolitical interests against a rising China whereas it does not want to commit anything in relations to the challenge India faces from China and Pakistan at its territorial boundaries. The question whether the US has become more strategically relevant to India in dealing, for instance, with challenges at India's land frontiers or extremist religious ideologies unleashed by US policies in our region and West Asia, has not been asked. [22]

The current Indian dissatisfaction with US policy in Afghanistan, especially insofar as it implicates Pakistan, holds the potential for deepening New Delhi's grievances against Washington, particularly if the security environment in Afghanistan were to corrode beyond repair in the aftermath of the American withdrawal. [23] How are we "natural partners", when US and Indian policies towards Pakistan, Afghanistan and the Taliban differ. Are we natural partners when we question the wisdom of US military interventions in West Asia, its draconian sanctions on Iran that disrupt our energy security, and the policy of geopolitically weakening Russia to China's advantage. [24] Also New Delhi is worried that too visible an embrace of the United States might precipitate the very Chinese actions that the partnership is supported to guard against, especially when the strong interdependence in US-Chinese relations could circumscribe Washington's actions in support of India. [25] The simple question to be aired is what would be the US attitude in case of a war between India and China.

Second, the Indian concept of an inclusive-multilateral world order and adherence to independence in foreign policy decisions seriously limit the scope of a strategic partnership. The United States views international politics from the vantage point of a hegemonic power and remains determined to preserve its primacy. In contrast, India views the international system very much as a subordinate state and desires a multi-polar system that would more easily accommodate its preferences. Although this divergence may seem overly abstract at first sight, it nonetheless produces practical disagreements especially in regard to diplomatic cooperation over questions of global order. [26]

US blocks a greater role by countries like India in international political and financial institutions. Despite president Obama supporting India's effort to secure UN Security Council membership, nothing concrete has been done for India's inclusion. A realist estimate of American approach shows that the US does not want India to be included in the UNSC. On WTO and climate change issues, Indian and US views diverge as they look at them from different perspectives—from that of underdeveloped and developed countries respectively.

On account of independence in foreign policy, India is uncomfortable being too closely affiliated with the United States. According to Ashely J. Tellis, it may be due to its fears of entrapment in other US conflicts and its perception that partnering with Washington too visibly might compromise its claims to independence or its lack of confidence in the US willingness to come to its assistance in any future crisis with China. [27] It may also be because of the fact that India and the US being regional and global powers, it is futile to assume that India's interests can converge with that of the US in all important areas. [28] It shows that the differences between India and the US are fundamental and does fit a strategic relationship.

Third, competing economic interests, domestic concerns and political ambitions of both India and the US would naturally limit the deepening of the relationship into a strategic one. The best example for the competing business is the understanding on the liability provisions of the civilian nuclear deal. It shows that ultimately India has to give in, to protect US interests. The slow progress on the opening up of the Indian economy, differences on immigration issues, the special and strong Anglo-Saxon and Western understanding on world affairs, US meddling in South Asia etc. are pointers to the fact that there many potential limitations to Indo-US relations. It is questionable how India and US can be natural allies when they differ on policies towards Pakistan, Afghanistan the Taliban. [29]

Hyping-up our relations with the US reduces our political space to criticize its actions when we disagree. A case in point is Obama's objectionable lecture to us on religious freedom and his pointed reference to Article 25 of our Constitution, which is a controversial domestic issue in India. [30] India also has strong objections to the tightening immigration policies in the US.

Is Indo-US Relationship a Strategic Partnership?

Depending on the range, nature and comprehensiveness, Indo-US relationship is described as a strategic partnership. In the globalised context of intensive interconnectedness, branding relationship as strategic merely based on connectivity would be a misnomer. To understand this one must know what are strategic partnerships and alliances.

Concept of Strategic Relationship: The concept of strategic relations goes beyond the normal kind of friendship or cooperation between parts. It refers to a comprehensive understanding between two or more countries on a wide variety of core bilateral and multilateral spheres that can serve the long-term interests of the countries concerned on a long-term or permanent basis. [31]

The Routledge Encyclopaedia of Political Economy understands strategic partnerships as a kind of relationship, which "involves two actors that are powerful and capable of taking strategic action together". [32] Strong political and cultural bonds are required for a strategic relationship to take off and flourish. Strategic partnership is one that both parties regard as important to achieve their core goals. [33] Presence of common values, common interests, mutual understanding and constructed identities are essential criteria for a 'partnership', as opposed to mere 'co-operation'. It could furthermore be argued that a prerequisite for a proper 'partnership' is that it must be between generally similar parties of roughly equal size. In strategic relationship, military dimension of the relationship is given greater importance.

Nature of Alliance: An important aspect of strategic partnership is the nature of alliance. There are different types of alliances. Tactical alliances are perhaps the most straight forward form of state alignments. The primary purpose of a tactical alliance is to counter an immediate threat or adversary that has the potential to challenge a state's most vital interests. Tactical alliances are instrumental and often opportunistic in nature as they allow states to address a pressing and urgent issue. Leaders usually justify them on the basis of conditions on the ground and by the imperatives of realpolitik. [34]

Historical alliances are enduring partnerships that sustain in spite of significant ruptures or changes in the international system. The structural features of such an alliance, which outlast time- or threat-specific contingencies, empower allies to sustain cooperation, relying on past successes as focal points to justify additional partnerships. Historical allies tend to accept short-term compromise that may not be fully congruent with national interests, in the hope that they will obtain some benefits in the longer run. Such a trade-off is impossible within the framework of a tactical alliance. They differ from tactical alliances because of their ability to redefine their purpose in spite of a significant structural change in the international landscape that would have rendered a tactical alliance moot. An instance of a historical partnership is the relationship between UK and the US. [35]

The concept of natural alliances goes beyond partners' shared sense of history by additionally hypothesizing commonalities in political culture and in narratives about how the world works or should work. These commonalities adapt to the new landscape through a constant reconstruction of the identities of natural allies who seek to tell or retell history to better face the present and to adjust to the future. Existing ties and institutions that formalized the relationship allow the alliance to self-sustain and strengthen over time. A natural alliance is therefore resilient and is likely to better resist exogenous shocks, though these may affect it in the short-run. It does not exclude disagreements and tensions, but reduces the likelihood of misunderstandings in the long-run. [36]

A Sceptical Relationship: Despite the so called strategic partnership, US and India are very sceptical about each other and do not trust beyond a level. The US complaint is that India has not been strategically reciprocal. The nuclear liability law that denied US suppliers nuclear business in India for some time is cited as an example. The idea of strategic partnership, security architecture and military alliances contradict India's basic foreign policy precepts. Even after the end of Cold War and the post-Cold War shift in India's foreign policy priorities, the traditional impulses of an independent course in foreign policy and aversion to military and security alliances are still very strong. India had not been a party to and is not used to any military and strategic alliances.

There is no understanding as to what extent and degree they need each other. India believes that US needs India more than ever. India thinks that the US wants India for the preservation of the balance of power in Asia, enhancing American competitiveness and enlarging its markets through deepened linkages with a growing Indian economy, thereby strengthening the American vision of a concert of democratic states by incorporating a major non-Western exemplar of success such as India. India is deeply suspicious of the American moves as it fears that it would convert India into an American stooge and would get implicated in unnecessary conflicts.

Moreover, India is not sure of whether it would get any

military assistance from the U.S. in case of a war with its traditional adversaries—Pakistan and China. These scepticisms are because of the reality that the Indo-US relations are at best a tactical alliance and not a strategic partnership.

Conclusion

The talk of a new relationship between India and the US is the result of the emergence of China as a challenger to American hegemony. Most of the factors that have been identified and highlighted as shared values and principles were present ever since India became independent in 1947. But these factors could not strengthen the bilateral relationship because of the underlying geopolitical and strategic discords in the context of the interplay of Cold War equations. Looking at the history and evolution of Indo-US relations, the relationship is more in the category of friendly-tactical relationship born out of contemporary compulsions of international politics. It is neither a natural alliance nor a strategic partnership or a historical partnership.

At best it is tactical alliance. India and the United States are still some distance away from realizing their objective of cementing a strong geopolitical affiliation that promotes each other's vital interests. The primary objective of US relations is to prevent Chinese ascendancy in global politics by promoting Indian ambition for great power status that would ensure regional stability in Asia and protect the geopolitical interests of the US. Since both India and the US are motivated by their own self-interests, the friendly relationship between the two is likely to continue but will be marred by the fundamental differences and is unlikely to turn into a strategic one in the foreseeable future. There is no set pattern or understanding in the engagement. Therefore, the so called partnership is left to the vagaries and oscillations of bilateral and other hiccups.

Endnotes

1. C.A., Josukutty (2015), "Democracy Promotion by India and US in the Af-Pak Region: An Analysis", in Mohammed Badrul Aalam

(ed.), 'India and Her Neighbours: Towards a Proactive Partnership', New Delhi: Kaplaz Publications.

2. Kux, Dennis (1993), "Estranged Democracies: India and the United States", New Delhi: Sage Publications, pp. 447-448.
3. Indian Embassy (1998), "Speech of Atal Bihari Vajpayee at the Asia Society", September 28, New York, available at: http://www.indianemhassy.org/nspecial/cahinet/Primeminister/pm(asiasociety).htm.
4. U.S. Congressional Record (1998), "Proceedings and Debate of the 105th Congress Session", June 16, Senator Mack, United States Government Printing Office, Vol. 144, Part 9, Washington.
5. IDSA (2010), "India-United States 2020: United States, Europe, Nuclear Cluster", summary, Policy Brief 11, October 29, available at: http://idsa.in/policybrief/IndiaUnitedStates2020.
6. Singh, Manmohan (2005), "Address to the Joint Session of the United States Congress", July 19, Washington D.C., reproduced in *Seminar*, No. 560, April 2006.
7. Rice, Condoleezza (2005), "U.S.-India Civilian Nuclear Cooperation Agreement", Testimony Before the House International Relations Committee, April 5, Washington, available at: http://www.state.gov/secretary/rm/2006/64146.htm.
   Burns, Nicholas R. (2007), "America's Strategic Opportunity with India", *Foreign Affairs*, Vol. 86, No. 6, p. 145.
8. "US Secretary of State Address Press Conference in New Delhi" (2005), *Hindustan Times*, transcript, March 16.
9. Armitage, Richard L., Burns, R. Nicholas and Fountain, Richard (2010), "Natural Allies, A Blueprint for the Future of U.S.-India Relations", Centre for New American Security (Report), available at: http://www.cnas.org/files/documents/publications/CNAS_Natural%20Allies_ArmitageBurnsFontaine.pdf#page=1&zoom=auto,0,792.
10. Armitage, Richard L., Burns, R. Nicholas and Fountain, Richard (2010), op. cit.
11. Green ,F. Michael and Twining, Daniel (2008), "Democracy and American Grand Strategy in Asia: The Realist Principles Behind an Enduring Idealism" , *Contemporary Southeast Asia*, Vol. 30, No. 1, p. 9.
12. Raja Mohan, C. (2006), "Crossing the Rubicon: The Shaping of

India's New Foreign Policy", New York, Palgrave Macmillan; in Chellaney, Brahma (ed.), 'Asian Juggernaut: The Rise of China, India, and Japan', New Delhi: Harper Collins.

13. Shrivastav, Sanjeev (2016), "Obama: The US President's Legacy on US-India Ties", May 19, available at: http://thediplomat.com/2016/05/goodbye-obama-the-us-presidents-legacy-on-us-india-ties.
14. C. Raja Mohan (2007), "Balancing Interests and Values: India's Struggle with Democracy Promotion", *The Washington Quarterly*, Vol. 30, No. 3, pp. 99-115.
15. Shrivastav, Sanjeev, op. cit.
16. Ibid.
17. Rama Lakshmi (2016), "India and U.S. Deepen Defence Ties with Landmark agreement", August 30, available at: https://www.washingtonpost.com/world/india-and-us-deepen-defense-ties-with-landmark-agreement/2016/08/30/2e7e045b-e3c3-49ff-9b2c-08efaa27b82b_story.html.
18. "U.S.-India Security and Defence Cooperation", Centre for Strategic and International Studies, available at: https://www.csis.org/programs/wadhwani-chair-us-india-policy-studies/past-india-chair-projects/us-india-security.
19. Ashely J. Tellis (2015), "Endowment for International Peace, Unity in Difference Overcoming the US-India Divide", Carnegie Endowment for International Peace.
20. Iqbal Anwar (2015), "US Hands Over Used Combat Aircraft, Other Weapons", May 7, available at: https://www.dawn.com/news/1180506.
21. Iqbal Anwar (2015), "US Approves Billion-dollar Arms Sale to Pakistan", April 8, available at: http://www.dawn.com/news/1174606.
22. Sibal, Kanwal, "India must be hard-headed on US relations" (2015), February 9, available at: http://www.dailymail.co.uk/indiahome/indianews/article-2946592/India-hard-headed-relations.html.
23. Ashely J. Tellis, op. cit.
24. Sibal, Kanwal, op. cit.
25. Ashely J. Tellis, op. cit.
26. Schaffer, Teresita C. (2009), "India and the United States in the 21st Century", Center for Strategic and International Studies, Washington D.C.: and Perkovich, George, (2010) "Toward

Realistic U.S.-India Relations," Carnegie Endowment for International Peacc, Washington D.C., available at: http://carnegieendowment.org/files/realistic_us_india_relations.pdf.

27. Ashely J. Tellis, op. cit.
28. Srinath Raghavan (2015), "Modified' Foreign Policy Interrogating Coherence, Finesse, Efficacy", *EPW,* January 31, Vol. L, No. 5, pp. 10-11.
29. Sibal, Kanwal, op. cit.
30. Sibal, Kanwal, op. cit.
31. Emerson, Michael (2001), "The Elephant and the Bear: The European Union, Russia and their Near Abroad", Archive of European Integration, p. 45, available at: http://aei.pitt.edu/32565.
32. Jones, R.J. Barry (2001), The Routledge Encyclopaedia of Political Economy, first edition, available at: http://www.routledgeonline.com/politics/Book.aspx?id=w053.
33. Vahl, Marius (2006), "A Privileged Partnership? EU-Russian Relations in a Comparative Perspective", DIIS Working Paper, No. 3., available at: https://www.econstor.eu/bitstream/10419/84582/1/DIIS2006-03.pdf.
34. Ghez, Jeremy (2011), "Alliances in the 21st Century: Implications for the US-European partnership" , Rand Corporation , occasional papers, p. viii, available at: http://www.rand.org/content/dam/rand/pubs/occasional_papers/2011/RAND_OP340.pdf.
35. Ibid.
36. Ibid.

11

India's Soft Balancing with US and China

Anil Kumar P.

Balancing the strategic alliance with the US and strategic competition with China is the most vital task and test for India's foreign policy in recent times. The idea of resisting the stronger one and maximising the national interest touches upon the work of political realists of this 21st century. They argue that states in the post-Cold War era balancing against the unipolar might or the stronger one is not in the traditional sense of using military build-ups, war-fighting alliances, or transfers to military opponents. Instead it is through "soft balancing", in which states leverage international institutions, economic statecraft, and diplomatic arrangements to counterbalance the hegemony of the competitor. [1] New Delhi's proactive engagement with US, China, Japan and Russia suggests a more sophisticated and interest-based foreign policy than that gauged simply from the optics.

With the demise of Soviet Union, United States emerged as the lone super power in this world. It leads to the decline of classical balance of power system. In this context, a paradigm shift has occurred in India's relations with great powers. Regarding India-US Relations, it has moved from 'estrangement' to 'engagement'. According to Venu Rajamony and John Graver, India-China relations are on a definite path of improvement and their trade relations are bettering day by day. [2] Now, India is expanding business and defence co-operation with Russia and Japan. But the major powers like US and China are concerned that they have some strategic interest in dealing with India and many of their interests are conflicting in nature. It provides ample opportunities for India to bargain with them through the policy of soft balancing.

This article narrates the concept of soft balancing and analyses how India is in soft balancing with US and China. It also explores the strategic options India is pursuing in its policy of soft balancing and the challenges it faces in this context. The core argument of this chapter is that in the midst of this co-operation, competition and conflict, India is pursuing a realist soft balancing strategy. The countervailing power dynamics are playing in subtle way in this soft balancing. It is not only a product of specific configurations of the power distribution in the system but also a rational behaviour under different conditions of dependence. Interplay between power disparity, compelling international situation and strategic, technological and economic dependence shapes a state's decision in choosing different balancing strategies. The higher the power disparity and dependence, the more likely a state chooses soft balancing to pursue its security. The huge power gap, compelling international situation and increasing strategic, technological and economic interdependence between India, United States and China shape soft balancing in their mutual relations.

Soft Balancing

It was a mistake to expect hard balancing to check the power of the international system's strongest state, a growing number of analysts maintain, because, under unipolarity, countervailing power dynamics first emerge more subtly in the form of *soft balancing*, as it is typically known. [3] T.V. Paul provides a concise definition of this basic concept.

"Soft balancing involves tacit balancing short of formal alliances. It occurs when states generally develop ententes or limited security understandings with one another to balance a potentially threatening state or a rising power. Soft balancing is often based on a limited arms build up and ad hoc co-operative exercise or collaboration in regional or international institutions; these policies may be converted to open, hard balancing strategies if and when security competition becomes intense and the powerful states becoming threatening". [4]

The most serious theoretical effort to fully develop the *soft balancing* concept is offered by Robert A. Pape. In his article *Soft Balancing Against the United States,* he advances three propositions that challenge the prevailing view that major powers cannot balance against the strongest one (here he mentions about United States). [5] *First,* the Bush's strategy of aggressive unilateralism changed the United States long enjoyed reputation for benign intent and giving other major powers reason to fear its power.

Second, major powers are already engaging in the early stages of balancing behaviour against the United States. In the near term, France, Germany, Russia, China, Japan, India, and other important regional states are unlikely to respond with traditional hard balancing measures, such as military build-ups, war fighting alliances, and transfer of military technology to US opponents. Directly confronting US preponderance is too costly for any individual state and too risky for multiple states operating together, at least until major powers become confident that members of a balancing coalition will act in unison. Instead, major powers are likely to adopt *soft balancing* measures: that is, actions that do not directly challenge US military preponderance but that use non-military tools to delay, frustrate, and undermine aggressive unilateral US military policies. Soft balancing is always using international institutions, economic statecraft, and diplomatic arrangements for its measures for its effective functioning.

Third, soft balancing is likely to become more intense if the dominant state continues to pursue an aggressively unilateralist strategy.

A growing body of international relations literature contends that balance of power theory has become relic of the Cold War. [6] According to this literature, second ranking major powers such as Russia and China are abandoning balance of power strategies despite increased US capabilities in almost all parameters of traditional sources of national power. [7] In every category of new weapons development and acquisition, the United States is widening its lead vis-à-vis the rest of the world. Not only does it possess global power status, but it has also been pursuing unilateralist strategies to prevent the rise of a peer competitor. Since the terrorist strikes of September 11, 2001 'preventive' and 'pre-emptive' military actions against regional challengers seeking weapons of mass destruction have become key part of the United States global strategy. [8]

Since the end of Cold War, second tier major powers such as China, France, Germany, India and Russia have mostly abandoned traditional hard balancing, based on countervailing alliances and arms build-up at the systematic level. This does not mean, however, that they are helplessly watching the resurgence of US power. These states have forgone military balancing primarily because they do not fear losing their sovereignty and existential security to the reigning hegemony, a necessary condition for such balancing to occur. In the past, weaker states aligned themselves against increasing power of a hegemonic state out of concern that the rising power would inevitably challenge their sovereign territorial existence.

The US imperial strategy by indirect methods sufficiently assures these powers that they are safe from predatory attacks by the United States. Indeed, they view the United States as constrained hegemon whose power is checked by a multitude of factors including international democratic institutions, domestic politics, and above all, the possession of nuclear weapons by some second ranking powers. In this new environment they have also begun to engage in soft balancing, which involves the formation of limited diplomatic coalitions or entents, especially at the United Nations, with the implicit threat of upgrading their alliances if the United States goes beyond its stated goals. [9]

According to T.V. Paul, soft balancing occurs under the following conditions:

1. The hegemon's power position and military behaviour are

of growing concern but do not yet pose a serious challenge to the sovereignty of second tier powers.

2. The dominant state is a major source of public goods in both economic and security areas that cannot simply be replaced.
3. Dominant state cannot easily retaliate because they do not directly challenge its power position with military means. [10] While pursuing soft balancing, second tier states could engage the hegemon and develop institutional links with it to ward off possible retaliatory actions. In the post-Cold War era, soft balancing has become an attractive strategy through which second tier major powers are able to challenge the legitimacy of the interventionist policies of the United States.

The Strategy of *Soft Balancing*

Balancing is about equalising the odds in a contest between the strong and the weak. States balance when they take action intended to make it hard for strong states to use their military advantage against others. The goal can be to deter a strong state from attacking or to reduce its prospects of victory in war. Traditional hard balancing seeks to change the military balance in an actual or (more often) potential conflict by contributing military capabilities to the weaker side through measures such as a military build-up, war-fighting alliance, or transfer of military technology to an ally. [11]

How *Soft Balancing* Works?

States can also seek to equalise the odds through soft balancing. Balancing can involve the utilisation of tools to make a superior state's military force harder to use without directly confronting that state's power with one's own forces. Although soft balancing relies on non-military tools, it aims to have a real, if indirect, effect on the military prospects of a superior state. Mechanisms of soft balancing include territorial denial, entangling diplomacy, economic strengthening, and signalling of resolve to participate in a balancing coalition. [12] All of these steps can weaken the military power that the superior state can bring to bear in battle.

Territorial Denial: Superior states often benefit from access to the territory of third parties as staging areas for ground forces or as transit for air and naval forces. Denying access to this territory can reduce the superior state's prospects for victory, such as by increasing the logistical problems for the superior state or compelling it to fight with air or sea power alone—constraints that effectively reduce the overall force that a stronger state can bring to bear against a weaker one.

Entangling Diplomacy: Even strong states do not have complete freedom to ignore either the rules or procedures of important international organizations or accepted diplomatic practices without losing substantial support for their objectives. Accordingly, states may use international institutions and ad hoc diplomatic manoeuvres to delay a superior state's plan for war and thereby reduce the element of surprise and give the weaker sides more time to prepare; delay may even make the issue irrelevant. Especially if the superior state is also a democracy, entangling diplomacy works not only by affecting the balance of military capabilities that can be brought to bear in the dispute but also by strengthening domestic opposition to possible adventures within the superior state.

Economic Strengthening: Militarily strong, threatening states that are the targets of balancing efforts usually derive their military superiority from possession of great economic strength. One way of balancing effectively, at least in the long-run, would be to shift relative economic power in favour of the weaker side. The most obvious way of doing this is through regional trading blocs that increase trade and economic growth for members while directing trade away from non-members. If the superior state can be excluded from such important blocs, its overall trade and growth rates may suffer overtime.

Signals of Resolve to Balance: Second-ranked powers seeking to act collectively against a sole superpower confront intense concern that the needed collective action may not materialize. Soft balancing, in addition to its direct usefulness in restraining aggression by a unipolar leader, may also address this problem by helping to coordinate the expectations of mutual balancing behaviour. If multiple states can cooperate, repeatedly, in some of the types of measures listed above, they may gradually increase their trust in each other's willingness to cooperate against the unipolar leader's ambitions. Thus, a core purpose of soft balancing is not to coerce or even to impede the superior state's current actions, but to demonstrate resolve in a manner that signals a commitment to resist the dominant power's future ambitions. Accordingly, the measure of success for soft balancing is not limited to whether the dominant power abandons specific policies, but also includes whether more states join a soft balancing coalition against the unipolar leader.

Soft Balancing with US and China: India's Strategic Options

A soft balance of power system involving many countries can be envisaged as one in which each country tries to be the balancer, promoting its own interest by building relations with both countries, even as it engages in selective collaboration with one or the other on an issue by issue basis. In such a system, none of the countries would enter into any formal alliances with the others. Each country tries to expand relations with the other. At the same time, where interests converge and few countries find themselves on the same side, they do not hesitate to work together to advance their common interest.

The competing and conflicting relationship between US and China and the strategic relationship of India with both provides ample opportunities for India in maximizing the benefits through co-operation. India is engaging with these powers through soft balancing in this context. Any kind of hard balancing against these powers will affect India's interest because of the conflicting and competing nature of relationship between the US and China. India is not interested in creating troubles in their relations with US and China. Most often they have conflicting and competing interests. It is important to note that current trends in India-US relations are not vehemently opposed by China in an open manner. In agricultural and environmental issues, India and US have conflicting positions.

Regarding environmental issues, India and China have common perspectives and they stand against the position of the United States. Most of the nations in South Asia, and US have similar position on terrorism. India and Pakistan whole-heartedly supported the US war against terrorism. Interestingly, Sino-Indian relations are not free from disruptions. Border issues, Tibetan problems, Chinese support to Pakistan etc. are major grey areas in bilateral relations. But on energy security and trade, both have mutual interests.

The realization of the Indo-US Civilian Nuclear agreement, renewal of the Strategic Framework Agreement with Modi government, Joint Naval exercise and the US support for India for the UN Security Council and "Make in India" programme are different strategic avenues before India for strengthening their co-operation. At the same time, it creates a soft balancing against the emerging power China and keeps option open for China to nurture a beneficial relationship with US and India. On many multilateral forums, India and China are joining together to keep their interest.

Soft balancing also provides more strategic options to India to have fruitful relations with countries like Japan, which are not liked by either US or China. Areas of energy co-operation, alliances in counter terrorism efforts and technological co-operation are certain strategic options for India. In the coming decades, India will have to devote much attention to the creation and maintenance of an optimal India-China-US triangle. But it is a fair assumption that the American concern about China's emergence as a rival power, and China's keenness to ensure that India does not become an active member of a US-led China containment policy, will ensure that a self-confident "rising" India will not be without diplomatic options. All in all, India and US must reduce trust deficit with China to ensure better understanding of each other's strategic intentions so that policies are not based on the assumption that the worst case scenario is a probable one.

One of the most important options before India in its soft balancing with US is its military co-operation rather than military alliance. In addition to this, the technological co-operation—especially in the space programme—co-operation in counter terrorism and strengthening of trade relations are the major options before India in this effort.

Indo-US and Sino-Indian relations are qualitatively different. It is true that there are some very important issues, like sanctity of national sovereignty, climate change, international trade and finance rules, multi-polarity, etc., where India and China would find themselves on the same side of the debate; but the fact is, Indo-US relations have different dynamics, based on the two countries' shared democratic political systems and values, viz. pluralism, tolerance, openness and respect for fundamental freedoms and for human rights. Further differentiating Indo-US and Sino-Indian relations is the presence of a huge Indian Diaspora in US. Many would argue that in the long-run, India and US have a strong congruence of interests in managing the rise of China. [13]

The US interest in South Asia is visible in history. They are very keen in building a strategic partnership with India. The US interest is to use India against the emerging China. A failed Pakistan is not fulfilling their target and that is also a compelling factor. In the case of strategic security of China, better relations with South Asian countries are necessary. China's *string of pearl strategy* [14] and investment diplomacy is important in this context.

The Sino-US competing interests in South Asia really opened many chances for India to bargain with these major powers. Hence, India has started to take up issue by issue decisions on a priority basis and they are playing soft balancing in this context.

The strategic options of India's soft balancing against US and China could be summarised as follows:

1. Find the areas of convergence between India's interest with US and China and bettering the relationship and co-operation in those areas of convergence in an effective manner.
2. Foster economic co-operation and strengthen trade relationship effectively in this globalised era in a mutually benefiting manner.
3. Strengthen limited arms build-up, informal, tacit or ad hoc security understandings and military co-operation to fight against terrorism and to address the common security concerns through a co-operative security framework.
4. Find the countries which are strategically important in India's balancing against United States and China and use them effectively. India can use alliance with the countries like Japan, Russia, Australia, Vietnam etc. in this effort of balancing against US and China.
5. India can even use United States and China on its balancing against each other because both these major powers are competing with each other for making allies all around the world. This provides opportunity for India to bargain with both.
6. India can also use multilateral forums like UN and regional organisations like ASEAN, BRICS, SAARC etc., as a platform to find allies in its efforts of balancing with major powers on international issues like environmental problems, terrorism and other common comprehensive security threats.

India's *Soft Balancing*: Challenges

The success of India's soft balancing against US and China is dependent on the co-operation of India with the countries which are significant in its balancing strategy. The inconsistency in foreign policy and the benefit India can offer to other countries in this effort are always a matter of concern. India can use alliance with countries like Japan effectively in its soft balancing strategy. But its lack of attention in building and strengthening relationship with those kinds of natural allies are still a problem. Even though India is a major power in South Asia, neighbouring countries are better satellites for China and US. China is heavily investing in the economies of smaller South Asian countries and thus creating deep inroads into the region. US-China competition for strategic allies all over the world creates ample opportunities for India, but at the same time it provides them with a lot of other choices and this is a strategic concern for India in many ways, especially in the South Asian context.

Regarding India's soft balancing against China, a two-pronged China policy is required. On the one hand, India's strategic thinkers should carefully analyse China's moves which have the potential to adversely affect India's interests and take effective steps to safeguard these interests. On the other hand, it would be in India's interest to pursue areas of mutually beneficial engagement, both in a bilateral and in a multilateral framework. [15]

At the global level, the main issue would be how the growing power of China will be handled by the US. As Ashley Tellis puts it:

"The most important longer term challenge [for US] will be coping with the rise of China because this event portends the possibility of a consequential power transition at the core of the global system and, by implication, the displacement of US hegemony". [16]

What is emerging as US strategy is *congagement.* On the one hand, the United States seeks to lay down boundaries for China's rise by maintaining a favourable balance of power in Asia and, on the other, it engages it comprehensively. US's Asia pivot policy is a strategy in this direction.

While keeping the above facts, the probability is that the India-China-USA triangle is not likely, in the next couple of decades, to bring about any kind of alliance by the two against the third. A few years ago American scholar Harry Harding came to the conclusion that it is unlikely that the triangle will sufficiently shift to form an enduring alignment of two against the one. If it did, given the relative power of the three countries, it is most likely that the alignment would pit India and the United States against a more assertive China. But, he argued that such an arrangement is not in the American interest. Rather, Americans should prefer a triangle in which the United States can work together with both India and China to advance common interests. [17]

There are global challenges—proliferation of weapons of mass destruction, climate change, terrorism, piracy, narcotics, pandemics, etc. in which the three must work together. Clearly, each stands to gain if they co-operate to ensure safety of Sea Lines of Communication in the Indian Ocean. Sharing their strengths in research and development to meet growing danger of supply shortages of critical resources would seem a logical course to pursue as we move ahead in the 21st century.

In short, it is clear that soft balancing is not an easy task. Its success depends upon the ability of the state to bring the co-operation and support of other countries in their promotion and protection of national interest. Leadership, resources, soft and hard power capability are important in this context. Regarding India, its international image as a peace-loving country, the civilizational strength, stability of the economy it maintains and its flexibility and autonomy in the international arena are very important in its soft balancing with major powers like US and China.

Conclusion

Balancing India's alliance with US and China is one of the most important tasks for India in the 21st century. India's engagement with US and competition with China and the conflicting and competing Sino-US relations compels India to follow a different kind of strategic balancing in its engagement.

India has certain common concerns and divergences with both the major powers. The inherent conflict involved in the Sino-US relations and their search for allies all over the world give ample opportunities for India to bargain with both. The emerging comprehensive security threats, India's economic stability and strengthening soft power capability creates suitable grounds for India to maintain a soft balancing strategy in its relationship with US and China—which is beneficial for India in all the ways. There is also a possibility that if any of these powers raise a serious threat to India's security and interest, it would open the floor for hard balancing. Even though the trust deficit and the unequal engagement of China with India's neighbours are concerns, the mutual benefit India could attain from soft balancing strategy makes it an attractive option to be followed in the realist globalised era.

Endnotes

1. Robert A. Pape (2005), "Soft Balancing Against United States", *International Security*, summer, Vol. 30, No. 1, p. 10.
2. Venu Rajamony (2002), "India-China-US Triangle: A 'Soft' Balance of Power System in Making", available at: http://www.CSIS.org/Saprog/venu.pdf.
3. The best treatments of the general soft-balancing argument are Robert A. Pape, "Soft Balancing: How State Pursue Security in a Unipolar World", annual meeting of the American Political Science Association, Chicago, Illinois, September 2-5, 2004; Stephen M. Walt, "Keeping the World Off Balance", in Ikenberry (ed.) (2002), 'America Unrivalled: The Future of the Balance of Power', Ithaca, NY: Cornel University Press; T.V. Paul, "The Enduring Axioms of Balance of Power Theory", in Paul, James J. Wirtz and Michel Formann (eds.) (2004), 'Balance of Power Revisited', Stanford University Press, and in T.V. Paul (2005), "Soft Balancing in the Age of US Primacy", *International Security*, Vol. 30, No. 1, pp. 46-71. The most ambitious theoretical effort to fully develop the soft-balancing concept is of Robert A. Pape.
4. Stephen G. Brooks and William C. Wohlforth (2005), "Hard Times for Soft Balancing", *International Security*, summer, Vol. 30, No. 1, pp. 72-73.

5. Robert A. Pape (2005), "Soft Balancing Against United States", *International Security*, summer, Vol. 30, No. 1, p. 36.
6. T.V. Paul (2005), "Soft Balancing in the Age of U.S. Primary", *International Security*, summer, Vol. 30, No. 1, p. 46.
7. Ibid.
8. Preventive military action refers to engagement in a war before an adversary develops operational capabilities, thus forestalling future aggression. Pre-emptive action is meant to stop an attacker that is about to launch a war.
9. T.V. Paul (2005), op. cit., p. 47.
10. Ibid., p. 59.
11. Robert A. Pape (2005), op. cit., p. 36.
12. Ibid.
13. Vinod Khanna (2011), "India's Soft Balancing with China and the US in the Twenty-first Century", *Indian Foreign Affairs Journal*, Vol. 6, No. 3, July-September, pp. 293-304.
14. The *String of Pearls* theory is a geopolitical theory regarding potential Chinese intentions in the Indian Ocean region. It refers to the network of Chinese military and commercial facilities and relationships along its sea lines of communication, which extend from the Chinese mainland to Port Sudan.
15. Vinod Khanna (2011), op. cit., p. 302.
16. Ashley J. Tellis (2008), "Preserving Hegemony: The Strategic Tasks Facing the United States", in Ashely J. Tellis, Mercy Kuo and Andrew Marble (eds.), 'Strategic Asia 2008-2009: Challenges and Choices', Seattle and Washington D.C.: The National Bureau of Asian Research, p. 36.
17. Harry Harding (2004), "The Evolution of the Strategic Triangle: China, India and the United States", in Francine Frankel and Harry Harding (eds.), 'The India-China Relationship: Rivalry and Engagement', Oxford University Press.

12

India's Maritime Security: Some Observations

A. Subramanyam Raju

Introduction

There is strong linkage between human development and the seas. Historically, man has depended on the seas for his economic and social well-being. Sea has become important for a country's development. Sea provides unlimited repository of food (fish), natural resources, and fastest, cheapest and safest means to transport bulk goods. Coastal shipping has become an important means of moving goods across the country. Catching fish has become not only as a source of food but also as a source of income. Further, offshore gas and oil and mining are very important elements of national wealth and income. Coastal tourism contributes to income and provides employment in coastal areas.

India shares maritime border with all littoral countries of South Asia (Pakistan, Bangladesh, Sri Lanka and the Maldives), Indonesia, Thailand and Myanmar. It had delimited its maritime boundary with all its neighbours except with Pakistan. India has signed ten bilateral and three trilateral maritime agreements till date. [1] Indian Ocean has become very important for India's development. "To the other countries, the Indian Ocean is only one of the important oceanic areas; to India, it is a vital sea. Her lifelines are concentrated in that area, her freedom is dependent on the freedom of that coastal surface. No industrial development, no commercial growth, no stable political structure is possible for her unless her shores are protected", [2]

India's economy is largely dependent on foreign trade, most of which sails through the sea. India imports about two-thirds of its oil from the Gulf region and it imports natural gas and sulphur from West Asia and exports tea, tobacco, spices, vegetables, fruits, meat, jute, iron ore, engineering goods, leather, medicines, and defence equipment to West Asia. Under UNCLOS-III, nearly two million square kilometres of area has come under India's jurisdiction. India was recognized as a pioneer investor in ocean mining. India had been given the status of a pioneer nation in 1987 to explore and exploit the resources in the seabed and was allocated 150,000 sq. km of seabed by the UN Seabed Authority for mining in the central Indian Ocean which is only 240 miles away from Diego Garcia. [3]

There are 12 major ports (Chennai, Kochi, Ennore, Jawaharlal Nehru, Kolkata (including Haldia), Kandla, Mormugao, Mumbai, New Mangalore, Paradip, Tuticorin and Visakhapatnam), which have a capacity to handle over 740 million tons of cargo per year and account for about 58 percent of India's external trade shipped by sea. [4] Two new ports are being considered to be developed. A port at Dugarajapatnam, which is located 45 kilometres from Gudur and about 140 kilometres north of Chennai port. It is expected that the port will have a handling capacity of 50 million tons per annum, which would be the second major port in Andhra Pradesh after Visakhapatnam.

The other slightly larger port project and expected to have capacity of 54 million tons per annum is located at Sagar in West Bengal. Both the ports aim to triple the country's cargo-loading ability to 3.13 billion tons by 2020 through public-private-partnership (PPP). [5] Cargo traffic through ports was 976 million metric tonnes (MMT) in 2012 and is expected to reach 1,758 MMT by 2017. [6] Around 95 percent of India's trade by volume and 70 percent by value takes place through maritime transport. Indian Ocean is the third largest ocean with an area of 68.56 million square km. and is about twenty percent of the earth's surface. There are strategically important chokes in the region viz., Suez Canal, Strait of Hormuz, Bab-el-Mandeb, Cape of Good Hope, Straits of Malacca and Singapore, Sunda Strait and Lombok Strait.

However, only twenty percent of trade is conducted between the littoral states of the region and the rest eighty percent is by extra-regional states. In other words, it explains the interests and presence of the extra regional powers in the region. Thus, it became necessary for India to strengthen its navy to defend its economic and strategic interests. [7] The paper analyses India's policy towards maritime security.

Before Independence

Since the sixteenth century, the future of India has been determined not on the land frontiers, but on the oceanic expanse when the Indian Ocean has become the scene of a struggle for control of the sea. [8] For the past three centuries, it is evident "that any power which has unquestioned mastery of the sea and strength to sustain a land campaign can hold the Empire of India, monopolize her trade, and exploit her unlimited resource". [9]

During the rulers of Satavahana, Chola, Pallava, Chera and Pandyan, maritime strategy was adopted for prosperity and security of their kingdoms. [10] "The period of Hindu supremacy in the Ocean was one of complete freedom of trade and navigation...there was no interference of any kind with trade which was open to ships of all nations". [11]

However, during the later period, Great Moguls neglected the sea. On the sea, the Mughals were helpless and could not realize the importance of sea. Later down, the British, who ruled the country, did not enhance maritime activities from the Indian soil and discouraged Indians in ship building. Panikkar declares that "it may truly be said that India never lost her independence till she lost the command of the sea in the first decade of the sixteenth century". [12]

Viceroy of India (Lord Curzon) wrote to London about the importance to India of control of key choke points from the Horn of Africa to the Cape of Good to the Malacca Strait. But he was asked to mind his own business and leave the Royal Navy and their affairs to the authorities in London. [13] After its

Independence, due to resource constraints—economically poor and militarily weak; pursuing/practising ahimsa and non-violence (which dominated during the freedom struggle), keeping the armed forces at a distance and out of the policy decision-making and largely concentrating on keeping forces on Pakistani and Chinese borders—made India blind towards the maritime front and giving importance to land based resources.

Before India's Independence, K.M. Panikkar, India's maritime strategist, argued that the Indian Ocean must remain "truly Indian", advocating the creation of a "steel ring" around India through the establishment of forward naval bases in Singapore, Mauritius, Yemen (Socatra) and Sri Lanka. [14] He maintained that "geography has been at all times one of the great and most regrettable gaps in Indian knowledge. Worse than even our lack of interest in historical things, has been our utter neglect of geography". [15] In his words, "The Peninsular character of the country and the essential dependence of its trade on maritime traffic give the sea a preponderant influence on its destiny...the economic life of India will be completely at the mercy of the power which controls the sea". [16]

He argued that since the sixteenth century, India has been facing a threat from the sea and it would continue to receive threats in future. He stressed the importance of protecting the maritime assets. Regarding India's need to develop its naval force in the region, he stated that India's security lies in the Indian Ocean, that without a well considered and effective naval policy, India's position in the world will be weak, dependent on others and her freedom at the mercy of any country capable of controlling the Indian Ocean. India's future, therefore, is closely bound with the strength it is able to develop gradually as a naval power. [17]

After Independence

Indian leaders in the beginning were occupied with continental mindset and could not go beyond Delhi and see the importance of maritime domain. Uday Bhaskar rightly argued that "The Himalyans loom large for Indian statesmen, while the oceanic expanses to the east and the west remain beyond the pale and comprehension of a parochial New Delhi". [18]

One of the reasons for our blindness, Prakash argues was "that as a nation we have been indifferent to the reading as well as writing of history". He further opined, "nowhere in any Western historical account does one find even a passing account of the seafaring skills of ancient Indians". Only the writings of Panikkar, "the lone Indian voice in this arena", have begun to redress this collective amnesia. [19] He maintained that the challenge before India is to "map its maritime heritage", combining the landward and seaward dimensions into a comprehensive mental map of the Indian Ocean region. [20]

Admiral Arun Prakash argues, "Regrettably, in India's case, we have historically suffered from an intellectual vacuum as far as strategic thinking is concerned, and that is why, after sixty years as a sovereign republic, we lack a clearly articulated statement of national aims and objectives. This is a cultural handicap which has not just deprived us of a healthy tradition of strategic debate and discourse, but also had a deleterious impact on internal security as well as foreign policy issues at the national level". [21]

India has not given adequate due to its navy. Though India's land border is about 9,900 miles, its sea frontier is 3,500 miles which is about one-third of that and its EEZ is about 2,013,410 square km., however, the allocation of budget to the Indian navy has been less.

As a littoral state, India initiated certain steps to promote peace in the region. It also had to protect the interests of people of Indian origin living in different parts of the region, viz., in Mauritius, the Reunion Islands and Seychelles. The external military presence in the region [22] posed not only a threat to the region, but also a major constraint on its role in the area. India has been enhancing its naval capabilities and presence in the region over a period of time.

Some of the littoral states perceived India's efforts to build a strong navy as its desire to play a big brother (not elder brother) role in the region. Although the Indian leaders have on many occasions explicitly stated that India is not aspiring for such a role, some littoral states continued to have doubts about India regarding its naval expansion plans and objectives. For instance, Sri Lanka felt that India, being a regional power, would like to dominate the region. [23] This sentiment was extremely strong in the 1980s. However, later on, a majority of littoral states in the Indian Ocean region gave up their apprehensions and consider India as a security provider.

India's Maritime Security

Security of India in the Indian Ocean has three dimensions: protect the east and west coasts of India and parts of the Arabian Sea and Bay of Bengal in support of ground and air operations ashore. Further, India needs to be more assertive in control of the Indian Ocean. "First, India needed to impose "complete or absolute control" over three hundred nautical miles of water out from India's coastline to defend the homeland, the exclusive economic zone, and offshore islands. Second, the navy had to exert "moderate control" over an ocean belt extending some three to six hundred nautical miles from Indian coasts in order to secure its sea lines of communications and provide situational awareness. Finally, the navy needed to exercise "soft control", power projection and deterrent capabilities, beyond seven hundred nautical miles from Indian shores". [24] The Andaman-Nicobar archipelago has 244 islands, which is considered to be a "metal chain" that could prevent the passage through the Malacca Strait.

After the liberalization process had taken place and maritime threats which became obstacles to safety of freedom of navigation, India realized the importance of becoming a maritime power. India has been expanding its presence in the region particularly in the choke points. According to the Indian Navy's 2004 Maritime Doctrine, "Control of the choke points could be useful as a bargaining chip in the international power game, where the currency of military power remains a stark reality". [25] Along the Arabian Sea coast, a new seaport and naval air station at Karwar was built, which would help to advance the navy's "blue water capabilities". India is also building a naval patrol base in the Lakshadweep Islands, which would control of the area closer to the Nine Degree Channel choke point. India has developed a naval base in the Andaman and Nicobar islands also.

Indian Maritime Doctrine, 2004, describes maritime strategy of India largely as a function of economic development and prosperity. "India's primary maritime interest is to ensure national security. This is not restricted to just guarding the coastline and island territories, but also extends to safeguarding our interests in the [exclusive economic zone] as well as protecting our trade. This creates an environment that is conducive to rapid economic growth of the country. Since trade is the lifeblood of India, keeping our SLOCs (sea lines of communication) open in times of peace, tension or hostilities is a primary national maritime interest". [26]

Realising the importance of geography, the document states that "by virtue of our geography, we are…in a position to greatly influence the movement/security of shipping along the SLOCs in the [Indian Ocean Region] provided we have the maritime power to do so. Control of the choke points could be useful as a bargaining chip in the international power game, where the currency of military power remains a stark reality". [27]

In its maritime strategy, India states explicitly that it will strive to ensure the safety of the Ocean's sea lines of communications: "Our strategy recognizes that the sea lines of communication passing through our region are critical for our economic growth and of the global community. Smaller nations in our neighbourhood as well as nations that depend on the waters of the Indian Ocean for their trade and energy supplies have come to expect that the Indian Navy will ensure a measure of stability and tranquillity in the waters around our shores". [28]

It has been arguing for absence of extra regional powers'

presence in the Indian Ocean region. Being a developing state, it has been arguing for greater autonomy. One can understand that a weak state always seeks to have autonomy. However, later in the post-Cold War period, India has been widening its security front. Now, it needs to become a player to maintain law and order and should give up seeking autonomy. India's task should be management of the international order and not seeking autonomy from it. India has to shift its policy from rule taker to rule maker and stakeholder. Indian navy's role should not only focus on India's security but also to take responsibility as a security provider. Indian navy has been assisting and supplying public goods for humanitarian relief and disaster assistance, search and rescue, and other related service during the 2004-05 tsunami relief operations and relief efforts following cyclone Nargis in 2008.

India has taken a number of steps in helping Mauritius operate a coast guard, strengthening Sri Lanka's ability to control its waters, or improving the ability of Mozambique, Madagascar, and Maldives to monitor their maritime domain. India was instrumental in conducting the Indian Ocean Naval Symposium in 2008 and membership is limited to regional states of the littoral. The symposium focused on the security of the Indian Ocean region. However, India has to shift away from the division between the regional and extra-regional since the US and China presence is inevitable in the region. [29] They have legitimate interests in the region, the way India has interests in the Pacific and South China Sea.

Is China a Threat?

India does perceive threat from China. China has been strengthening its presence in the Indian Ocean region. Pakistan, with the help of China, built the Gwadar port, which is one of the largest deep sea ports that will double Pakistan's sea trading capacity. India raised its concern over China's strategy in improving its links with Pakistan. It feels that its links with Pakistan particularly through this port, would pose a challenge to India's interest in the Bay of Bengal and in the

Arabian Sea, as it is expanding its naval presence in the Indian Ocean region. China has also assisted in the development of port facilities at Akyab, the Coco Islands, Cheduba and Bassein in Myanmar and Chittagong in Bangladesh. Through these facilities, China not only could protect its maritime energy transport routes during a crisis but can also control and dominate the sea lanes of communications of the region. India is uncomfortable the way China is expanding its naval presence around India.

Further, China is involved in constructing the first phase of Hambantota port in Sri Lanka. Sri Lankan government first approached and offered to India to construct the port. But due to reluctance from the private companies, the government did not show interest. Subsequently, the Sri Lankan government approached China and thus the later was awarded the contract to construct the port. Some of the security analysts argue that this port may be used by China to encircle India. Indian government should have encouraged the private companies by giving financial assistance as it is already involved in assisting Sri Lanka in various sectors.

The Hambantota port is located on a key shipping route and about 300 ships, mostly oil tankers, pass through it every day. The port was opened for international shipping in June 2012. The port provides docking and refuelling facilities to thousands of ships that sail oil and raw materials from Africa and the Persian Gulf to China. It is a crucial link in the "string of pearls" which China is building in the region through a network of ports to consolidate its economic and military influence in the Indian Ocean region.

Gotabaya Rajapaksa, Sri Lanka's former defence secretary, has justified China's increasing presence in the Indian Ocean saying that "the safety and stability of the Indian Ocean is critical for China's energy security and its increasing interest and increasing naval presence in this region is quite understandable". [30]

Further, China Satellite Communications Co. Ltd. (China

Satcom) and the state-owned China Great Wall Industry Corporation have been investing heavily in communication projects in India's neighbouring countries. Sri Lanka launching its first communication satellite with the Chinese help would be great threat to India's security. In 2012, a plot of land in the heart of Colombo earmarked for an Indian cultural centre (the Indian High Commission had completed all formalities) was sold to Chinese aircraft manufacturer, China National Aero Technology Import and Export Corporation. [31] India's national security agencies have expressed apprehension over these developments. Chinese footprints in Sri Lanka are visible both at the strategic and commercial levels. China's decision to send submarines in the Indian Ocean right up to the Gulf of Aden in the recent past has become an irritation for India.

Despite their differences, India and China have agreed to move ahead on other fronts. For example, the world's two fastest growing energy consumers agreed in January 2006 to cooperate on foreign energy exploration and development, even after India lost out to China on large energy projects in Angola, Myanmar, Ecuador, and Kazakhstan. That month India's state-run Oil and Natural Gas Corporation (ONGC) and the China National Petroleum Corporation jointly purchased assets in Syria's al-Furat oilfields for US$ 573 million. These two firms are already working together in Sudan's Muglad Basin to pump oil and construct a 940 mile pipeline to transport it to Port Sudan on the Red Sea. China is already India's second largest trading partner.

India and China do not have border dispute over maritime boundary. The two countries' navies conducted a bilateral exercise off the Kochi coast in the Arabian Sea in December 2005, but there have been no combined air or ground force manoeuvres yet. Since both have similar convergence of concerns over protecting sea lines of communications, on interruption of trade through sea, energy security etc., China and India should be good neighbours, good friends and good partners so that they can establish a strategic and cooperative partnership for peace and prosperity.

India's Engagements and Initiatives

India has been transcending its presence from South Asia to the rest of the world. It has actively participated in numerous initiatives to address various issues related to Indian Ocean. The IONS is one of them. India had been involved in hosting the IONS symposium in New Delhi in 2008 to promote a shared understanding of the maritime issues facing the littoral nation-states of the Indian Ocean and the formulation of strategies designed to enhance regional maritime security.

India has been conducting the biennial MILAN (togetherness) naval meetings since 1995 at Port Blair in the Andaman. In 2012, the five-day meet had fourteen participating countries including Australia, Bangladesh, Brunei, Indonesia, Malaysia, the Maldives, Mauritius, Myanmar, Sri Lanka, Thailand, Singapore and the Seychelles. This meeting was not a naval exercise but an opportunity to increase military-to-military relationships with the navies of regional states. Neither China nor the US was invited, probably to assert India's regional primacy.

India had 'Varuna' series of exercise with France in 2001 and conducted its first maritime exercise with the Japan in April 2007. It was announced that India would undertake its firsts ever exercises in the Atlantic Ocean, in concert with the British and French navies in 2008. It also had naval exercises with the US and China in the Indian Ocean.

India has been actively involved in the Indian Ocean Rim Association for Regional Cooperation (IOR-ARC) formed in 1997. The IOR-ARC was later renamed as Indian Ocean Rim Association (IORA). The aim of the association is to promote sustained growth and create common ground for regional economic cooperation.

India has been, in recent times, actively engaged with the littoral states through agreements to improve its relations with them. India has recognized the importance of the Indian Ocean, which was enunciated by Panikkar, before India obtained Independence from the British. India has been recognized as a security provider and gave consent by littoral states (including the majority of the Southeast Asian states) to enhance its naval presence in different parts of the region and in the Pacific Ocean. The present government has outlined its maritime policy: protecting mainland, island territories and its maritime interests; deepening partnership with littorals in the Indian Ocean region; enhancing multilateral cooperative maritime security in the region; promoting sustainable development in the region; and differentiating itself from the extra-regional powers. On the other hand, the government has sought to engage with other countries to maintain peace, tranquillity and security in the region.

Conclusion

Most of the maritime threats have transnational dimension and it is essential for India to have greater cooperation with neighbours on maritime security. Such cooperation may include measures such as joint naval patrolling, controlling of smuggling and pirate activities, and strengthening communication networks. Through cooperation, countries can improve ship building, weather forecasting, prevention of pollution and combating maritime terrorism. Apart from such measures, there is a greater potential for enhancing and institutionalizing economic cooperation in the exploration and exploitation of sea resources in the Indian Ocean waters.

Understanding of the maritime issues facing the littoral states of the Indian Ocean is essential to establish and promote transnational, maritime and cooperative mechanisms to mitigate maritime security concerns. The littoral states must develop interoperability (doctrines, procedures, organizational and logistic systems and operational processes) to identify areas of cooperation, which may be agreed upon. The Indian Ocean region is home to global terrorism, drugs and arms trafficking. The Golden Crescent on one side of India and the Golden Triangle on the other provides financial support for terrorist groups such as Al-Qaeda and Jemmiah Islamiah.

Hence, the areas such as the Horn of Africa, the Bay of Bengal and the Malacca Strait need to be protected otherwise they would become ungoverned areas. On the other hand, 100,000 ships travel through Indian Ocean each year carrying one-third of the world's bulk cargo, half of the container traffic and seventy percent of the global traffic of petroleum products.

About ninety percent of India's trade travels by sea. Some of its trade is being conducted through narrow straits at Hormuz, Malacca, and Babel Mandeb. Shipping through such straits is seen as most vulnerable in such waterways. It must be the driver of any security mechanism in the region. It needs to strengthen various multilateral frameworks to work towards bring peace, security and stability in the Indian Ocean. It has to strengthen cooperative security in the region. Being a larger littoral state and big stakeholder in the world trading system, India has to ensure "a measure of stability and tranquillity in the waters around its shores" for "[s]maller nations in its neighbourhood as well as nations that depend on the waters of the Indian Ocean for their trade and energy supplies". [32]

Endnotes

1. Bilateral agreements: Indonesia: August 8, 1974, January 14, 1977; Maldives: December 28, 1976; Myanmar December 23, 1986; Sri Lanka June 26, 1974, March 23, 1976 and November 22, 1976; Thailand June 22, 1978 and October 27, 1993; Bangladesh in 2014. Trilateral: Sri Lanka and Maldives July 24, 1976; Indonesia and Thailand June 22, 1978 and Myanmar and Thailand October 27, 1993.
2. K.M. Panikkar (1945), "India and the Indian Ocean: An Essay on the Influence of Sea Power on Indian History", London: George Allen & Unwin Ltd, p. 84.
3. Kenneth R. Simmondes (1988), "New Directions in the Law of the Sea", London: Oceana Publications, pp. 9 and 16.
4. UNCTAD (2013), "Review of Maritime Transport, 2013", New York: UN, p. 97, available at: http://unctad.org/en/publicationslibrary/rmt2013_en.pdf.
5. *The Hindu*, May 9, 2013, cited in UNCTAD, Ibid., p. 97.

6. "India in Business", Ministry of External Affairs, Government of India Investment and Technology Promotion Division, February 28, 2014, available at: http://indiainbusiness.nic.in/newdesign/index.php?param=industryservices_landing/361/2.
7. It has 2.015 million sq. km. of EEZ of which 30 percent lies in the region of the Andaman & Nicobar Islands. It was estimated that the stock of fish was between 50,000 and 100,000 tons in the area of 129,000 nautical sq. miles. It was estimated that 453,000 sq. km of EEZ contains about 40 million tons of fish and about one billion tones of oil. The West Coast region was estimated to have 570 oil-bearing structures, of which 176 have been confirmed and 81 discovered. See S.L. Rao, "Geopolitical and Economic Realities of the West Coast of India", in S.L. Rao (ed.), 'Indian Ocean: Challenges and Opportunities', New Delhi: Navy Foundation, 1992, p. 50.
8. Panikkar, n. 2, p. 7.
9. Ibid., p. 83.
10. Shiv Shankar Menon (2009), "Maritime Imperatives of Indian Foreign Policy", *Maritime Affairs*, Vol. 5, No. 2, winter, p. 16.
11. Panikkar, n.2, p. 35.
12. Ibid., p. 7.
13. Menon, n. 10, p. 16.
14. K.M. Panikkar (2010), "The Future of Southeast Asia: An Indian View", New York: The Macmillan Company, pp. 100-101, cited in David Brewster, 'An Indian Sphere of Influence in the Indian Ocean?', *Security Challenges*, Vol. 6, No. 3, spring, p. 16.
15. K.M. Panikkar (1955), "Geographical Factors in Indian History", Bombay: Bharatiya Vidya Bhavan, p. 17.
16. Panikkar, n. 2, p. 14.
17. Cited in Ibid., p. 92.
18. C. Uday Bhaskar (2008), "Crucial Maritime Space", *The Hindu*, September 16.
19. Arun Prakash (2009), "Historical Blunder", *Force*, New Delhi, July 2007, cited in James R. Holmes, Andrew C. Winner and Toshi Yoshihara, 'India Naval Strategy in the Twenty-first Century', London: Routledge, p. 14.
20. Holmes, Winner and Yoshihara (Ibid).
21. Arun Prakash (2007), "India's Maritime Strategy", *USI Journal*, Vol. 137, No. 568, April 1-June 30, pp. 157-176, cited in

Holmes, Winner and Yoshihara, n. 19, p. 9.

22. For further details, see A. Subramanyam Raju (2001), "Democracies at Loggerheads: Security Aspects of US-India Relations", Colorado: International Academic Publishers, and New Delhi: South Asian Publishers, pp. 75-100.
23. *Bangkok Post*, December 14, 1974.
24. 浪潮 [Lang Chao], "全景扫描印度海军—战略战术及战斗力" [A Complete Assessment of the Indian Navy: Strategy, Operations, and Combat Capabilities], 当代海军 [Modern Navy], July 2006, p. 41, cited in James R. Holmes and Toshi Yoshihara (2008), "China and the United States in the Indian Ocean: An Emerging Strategic Triangle?", *Naval War College Review*, Summer, Vol. 61, No. 3, p. 53.
25. Government of India (2004), "Indian Maritime Doctrine", Integrated Headquarters, Ministry of Defence (Navy), New Delhi, p. 64.
26. Government of India (2004), "Indian Maritime Doctrine", Integrated Headquarters, Ministry of Defence [Navy], New Delhi, April, p. 63.
27. Ibid., p. 64.
28. Government of India (2007), "Freedom To Use The Seas: India's Maritime Military Strategy", Integrated Headquarters Ministry of Defence (Navy), New Delhi, p. IV; (2010), "The Maritime Future of the Indian Ocean: Putting the G back into Great Power Politics", Hague Centre for Strategic Studies, September 13, p. 33.
29. C. Raja Mohan (2010), "India and the Changing Geopolitics of the Indian Ocean", *Maritime Affairs*, Vol. 6, No. 2, Winter, p. 6.
30. *Business Standard*, available at: http://www.business-standard.com/article/economy-policy/lankan-roulette-113032200472_1.html.
31. http://articles.timesofindia.indiatimes.com/2012-08-20/india/33287136_1_china-pakistan-prime-plot-galle-road.
32. Admiral Mehta (2009), Address to IISS, International Institute for Strategic Studies, 21 June 2007, cited in Geoffrey Till, "Sea Power: A Guide for the Twenty-First Century", London: Routledge, p. 333.

Index

Index

Govind